Diary of a Wimpy Eventer

Part One
How to get your leg over

The reader of this book, must only pick it up
if you've got an open mind and not too posh or too refined.

©2017 Victoria Brant – Diary of a Wimpy Eventer

www.wimpyeventer.com

The moral right of the author has been asserted
Printed in Great Britain.

Written, designed and produced by Gary and Victoria Brant
(Daddy Carrot and The Wimpy Eventer!)

Beautifully illustrated by Bonny Snowdon Fine Art

Cover printed by kind permission of the Thelwell Estate 2017 ©Thelwell Estate 2017
www.thelwell.org.uk

Edition 1
ISBN : 978-1-5272-0926-8

With thanks to...

There are so very many people who have influenced my life, who have made me who I am and keep me writing the way I do. I know I have an unusual talent, I am just grateful that I have been encouraged to let that talent fly.

To my darling Daddy Carrot who spends hours listening to chatter about horse boots, stable bedding preferences and which jumps I would like building next. He is a very nice human, one I am very proud to call my husband.

To my family who remain solid in the front of my mind throughout this journey, I will live closer very soon and see you much more often.

To my friends that supply wine, words and wisdom – that have proof read, course walked, supported me for years, I love you all.

To the wonderfully talented Bonny Snowdon for beautifully illustrating this book, her skills for capturing the very soul of my dear horse have touched me more than words can say.

And most importantly to the Diary of a Wimpy Eventer followers, without you this wouldn't exist. I wouldn't have been brave enough to ride let alone write. This is your achievement just as much as mine, I hope I have done you proud.

Love, as always
Vic and Pat
xxxx

GLOSSARY

Should you not have had a life of smelling like horse urine, there are probably a few terms within this book that might need further explanation...I have used my own terminology to help you understand those terms in the glossary below, these may or may not be factually correct!! Throughout the book, the first time they are used will be marked with a small heart.

- ♥ **Affiliated** – A category of competition that you pay to be a member of, usually means things run smoother resulting in less chance of death.

- ♥ **Arena** – A place that has a rubber floor and sometimes jumps and a gate that closes so that when you fall off, the horse can't escape.

- ♥ **Ascot Bloodstock Auctions** – An auction house where horses either for racing or that aren't very good at racing are sold to Joe Public.

- ♥ **Bravery Vest** – The Point Two Pro Air, a body warmer style arrangement that is clipped to your saddle which will inflate in less than a second if the cord is pulled!!! It will make you braver and safer.

- ♥ **Breakers and Youngsters** – young horses that you shouldn't ever get on unless you are experienced or foolish.

- ♥ **British Eventing (also referred to as BE)** – The affiliation name for the sport of eventing, also the name written on my car window sticker – I think it makes me look like a professional.

- ♥ **Calmer Syringe** – A tube of paste containing a herbal remedy that makes my horse less frisky.

- ♥ **Chip P*sser** – Someone that frequently sprays urine all over your good day/first place/clear round. They are people that indirectly say negative comments and make you feel like smearing faeces in their eyeballs.

- ♥ **Clear round** – When you don't knock any of the poles down or fall off or die whilst practicing the art of jumping.

- ♥ **Clinic** – Training sessions usually in groups of 3 or 4 where an instructor tells you how not to be so sh*t.

- ♥ **Combined Training** – This is a competition involving both a dressage test and show jumping round. Like eventing but with less death possibility.

- ♥ **Cross country (Also referred to as the death phase or XC)** The third phase of Eventing in which you cover yourself and your horse in layers of protective clothing and gallop as fast as you dare whilst jumping over obstacles that are 1. Big, 2. Solid and 3. Might well kill you.

- ♥ **Dressage** – The first phase of Eventing which is also a standalone sport. You and your horse dance inside an enclosed area having memorised the dance moves a few days before. You have the least chance of dying in this part.

- ♥ **Eventing** – Something that you should not do unless you are mad or rich or both. You will become hooked, poor and your chances of fatality will increase.
- ♥ **Field Master** – Someone that is in charge of how fast and how far you gallop when out hunting.
- ♥ **Gelding** – a male horse that has been removed of his man nuggets.
- ♥ **Hacking** – Riding your horse in any area that isn't an arena (e.g. roads, fields, paths, to the pub).
- ♥ **Hunter Trial** – A competition that is just the cross country element.
- ♥ **Hunting** – When a group of people and a pack of hounds run across the countryside chasing after the etiquette and morals of the 1940s. – They NEVER find them and usually return home p*ssed and covered in mud.
- ♥ **Livery yard** – a house share arrangement for horses.
- ♥ **Long reining and Lunging** – something you do when you are training horses or are too scared to ride them.
- ♥ **Mare** – a female horse.
- ♥ **Master Imp** – the Father horse of Pat. His semen has produced some of the best event horses of all time.
- ♥ **Medium Trot** – like regular trot (the up/down pace) only the horse stretches more and the rider loses more balance.
- ♥ **Minky** – Vagina.

- ♥ **Mrs. Mary King** – a VERY prolific and successful female event rider.

- ♥ **Neck Strap** – a band of leather tied around the horses neck that you can grab hold of if you feel like you might die.

- ♥ **Oxer** – a type of jump that is wider than just a single pole.

- ♥ **Prelim, Novice and Elementary** – Levels in dressage competitions – prelim being the easiest.

- ♥ **Rearing, Napping, Bucking and Bolting** – Things that horses do that terrify riders, these things are usually caused by humans and their lack of understanding.

- ♥ **Riding club** – usually a group of middle aged women that like wine, low key horse shows and chatter.

- ♥ **Rosette** – The Holy Grail of competitive riding, a large frilly badge that symbolises sweating, practice and non-death.

- ♥ **Schooling** – Teaching your horse to behave in a respectable manner by trotting around an arena pretending to be a professional and looking like 'you've got this'!

- ♥ **Schoolmaster** – a horse that has been 'schooled' so much it has given up the need to fight – he may even be safe for a non-rider/husband.

- ♥ **Sedalin Gel** – a syringe full of gel that you must get prescribed from the vet for sedating your horse.

- ♥ **Show jumping** – The sport of jumping clear over obstacles that will fall down if you breathe on them the wrong way. 4 penalties are issued if you knock one down, several penalties are issued if you stop to get your breath and go too slow!

♥ **Showing** – pruning your horse until it is basically bald in order for a judge to assess its suitable for the job.

♥ **Spooking** – The reaction a horse gives when he sees something that might well jump out and slit his throat, usually an upturned leaf, wheelie bin or crisp packet.

♥ **Start box (of doom)** – the area that you are imprisoned in before you are counted down to ride the cross country course.

♥ **Stock** – a type of tie that hides a double chin VERY well.

♥ **Tack** – a collective word for all of the things I buy and hide from my husband, namely saddles, bridles etc.

♥ **Trakehner** – (track-ay-ner) a type of cross country jump that looks okay from a distance but when you get near, has a huge gaping hole under it.

♥ **Vetting** – the process you can go through when buying a horse to see how many legs it is lame on.

♥ **Warmblood** – a type of horse usually a bit slow in the brain area but they make great jumpers and dressage horses.

♥ **Wasurk** – a Lincolnshire term for total pillock/arsebag/ knobhead/etc.

♥ **Wither** – the first bit of the horses spine after the neck that when you ride bare back, hurts your minky (see above).

INTRODUCTION

Ever wondered what it takes to over-come fear? To grab hold of something with both hands and never let go? Read on my dear friend; read on. I sit here and write this having come through the darkest tunnel, knowing full well what it takes to keep lifting your feet, even through the deepest clay. You don't even need to have touched a horse to know what it's like to feel consumed by self-doubt. Let go of everything just for a while, give yourself to this book and I guarantee you will feel less alone, more capable and laugh with me as I share my journey with you. You've got this, trust me, I've got your back.

IN THE BEGINNING

Growing up in rural Lincolnshire in the arse end of nowhere, there wasn't a lot else going on other than field sports and farming, my equestrian fate was almost inevitable. Neither of my parents encouraged the habit, none of my siblings appreciated the scent of horse urine either but it had me hooked from a very young age.

My father worked on the farm and my mother was the house keeper for the farm owners, salaries combined definitely couldn't fund a pony. I begged, stole and borrowed for any opportunity to stroke one, ride a Skegness beach donkey or gallop around the garden on Dobbin. Dobbin was my first horse. I was 5 years old and an early morning mystery tour of our farm cottage led me to him. Hidden under a blanket behind the living room door, as black as the night with a VERY rare white mane, there he was; my first pony. He was a little stiff to ride and his narrow wither♥ hurt my legs but I rode him every day for at least 4 years, jumping jumps and going on garden adventures until sadly I grew too big for him. His wooden pole was replaced and his paintwork touched up and he was handed down to other children for them to create their own magical memories on. My father had handmade Dobbin after work in the evenings. I can still remember the smell of paint on my pillow after I had tucked him up in my bed, my first horse – one I will NEVER forget.

At 18 after spending much of my youth hunting♥, showing♥ and pony clubbing on borrowed ponies and horses I dabbled in a bit of eventing♥ and I followed my heart to a small, private yard that offered the opportunity to compete 2 wonderful horses. I wasn't technically skilled in the dressage♥ arena or correctly positioned over a show jump but by golly I was brave as a lion going cross country♥. I was fearless, I would jump any fence, hedge or ditch from any stride and love every single second of flying through the air. That feeling of soaring over a huge log pile, landing with a thump and galloping away was what my dreams were made of. I was of course 18 and full of life. Hunting made me a plucky rider, throwing my heart over every jump and watching my horse follow, I hated standing around at the coverts getting cold but I loved the chase. The sound of the horn and the cry of the hounds, once it's in your blood, once you have breathed the scent of a frosty hunt meet, you will never let it go, it consumes you. This, it turns out was to be a pivot point in turning my life around.

Having got married far too young to a soldier in 2008, meant I left behind everything and everyone I had ever known for an Army posting 250 miles south of home. All of a sudden I was alone, living with a boy. I had no one for miles that I could call on, no-one to keep me sane. I had ridden all my life, it was all I knew, so I saved up £500 and went to Ascot Bloodstock Auctions ♥ to find myself a friend of the four legged kind.

Buying my first horse was one of the most exciting things I have ever encountered. I borrowed one of my husband's friends, hired a trailer and trundled off to a racehorse auction. Here I was, walking up and down lines and lines of thoroughbred horses that I couldn't even get out of the stables and watch them move let alone 'test ride'. I'll be honest, I had absolutely no clue what I was looking for! I think one that looked kind and 'non-bitey' was high on the list, preferably one that wasn't angrily gnawing on the door or kicking the cr*p out of the stable was also okay too. I chose a few geldings ♥ that looked okay, marked them in my catalogue and went into the bidding ring. I was terrified of bidding, the commitment and pressure of raising my number amongst people who were very experienced was more nerve wrecking than anything else. Incidentally they all sold for WAY more than my measly budget, after all I only had £500. It was raining outside, miserable, grey and I just wanted to go home, but boy I wasn't going home without a pony! In she came the sorry looking 4 year old mare♥. She had no name, she had no life in her eyes. The bidding dropped to a starting price of £350 and I couldn't believe my ears. I had to save this timid baby from the abattoir or worse, so in went my bid for £400. SOLD. Down went the gavel, a 16hh mare, fit and ready to ride, I called her India.

The next 2 hours spent getting that previously lifeless looking beast into the hired trailer were somewhat entertaining, she wasn't grateful for being saved at all! The next 18 months were much the same; spirited, but fun. India was a challenge to retrain but she was so bloody bold cross country that all was forgiven. Hunting my very own horse on Boxing Day was the best time of my life. Days seemed to drift away when we were together and because of her, I met some lovely new yard friends who are now life-long ones. I never really fell in love with her though, I couldn't put my finger on it. The expectation was too great for this first pony, it meant the reality only ever had one way to go.

As time with India slipped through my fingers, so did my marriage. I was lost. Getting married before I had worked out who I was, before I had grown into my own character turned out to be a terrible mistake. The huge age difference and the army lifestyle was taking its toll and I felt scared on more than one occasion. I was dependent and felt totally trapped. My unhappiness at home was rubbing off onto my horse and I made the decision to sell her. It wasn't at all as tough as it could have been. The most wonderful person turned up with the asking price and took her away. I knew my first baby would be very loved by her new mother and so I rested easy on that.

A BROKEN HOME, A BROKEN HEART

A few horseless months passed and I was growing increasingly fed up. Still treading the rocky road of my marriage, I needed a getaway, a distraction… I went looking for another horse, this time in the shape of a 4 year old warmblood♥.

I remember the day I bought Freckles like it was yesterday, I was so desperately excited and I couldn't wait to get him home. He looked like a rocking horse in the photos, perfectly dappled with the prettiest face. Who could have predicted what the day would turn into? On arrival, the grey lump was strolling around a muddy field, a field which then became a schooling♥ paddock. He was so very quiet in nature, immensely wobbly to ride and felt as though he was going to fall over at every turn, but what a soft look he had in his eye. I paid the money and loaded him up, just like that! He was £1200 – the most money I had ever spent on ANYTHING in my whole life.

We got 15 minutes into our 2 hour trip home on a dual carriage way when the trailer threw us sideways into the other lane. Our meaty 4x4 was being tugged and tossed about the road like a cat with a ball of wool. Never in a million years have I experienced anything quite so gut wrenching. What could have been going on in that trailer to cause such a kerfuffle in the car? We pulled onto the non-existent hard shoulder and I climbed out. All was still inside. I unbolted the small jockey door at the front left of the trailer and my heart jumped out of my throat. Out of the tiny door burst the blood stained grey fur of my new horses head. He had severely sliced an ear, but this was the least of my troubles. On second glance, not a single hoof was on the floor of the trailer. The poor sod had jumped over the breast bar and was suspended from it like a pendulum, crushing his head and neck against the front of the box. He was still but that look in his eye was sheer terror, one I hadn't see for many years. I very quickly pushed the bleeding head back in and closed the door to seek assistance.

The army training soldiers to remain calm and methodical in times of crisis was useful that day, my then husband climbed into the trailer and levered the poor horse upwards attempting to rock him backwards and free the breast bar that he was suspended from. It seemed like it was the best and only option until the poor frightened horse panicked. All of a sudden he had flipped, attempted to stand bolt upright, thrashing and banging with both of us still inside the trailer. He came crashing down onto his back, squashed this time between the back ramp and the separating partition. Everything went silent for what felt like an eternity. Was he dead? Unconscious? Could a horse lose consciousness? We left the trailer in the nick of time because the silence didn't last long. He was soon thrashing violently again trying to free himself from the metal bars of the partition that had enclosed his limbs. He was trapped.

On the grass verge, panic, fear and overwhelming emotion caused vomit to shoot up into my throat. I found the nearest motorway marker and called 999. Within 10 minutes, all lanes in both directions of the dual carriage way were empty. It was like a scene from a zombie apocalypse. Blue lights surrounded us very soon after.

The fire brigade were just amazing that day. A calm and confident chap jumped in with my petrified horse and soon Freckles was standing, his bleeding head hanging over the back door. We were escorted off the motorway and they cordoned off a pristine area of turf and opened the ramp. I glanced over at the entrance sign welcoming people into the Olympic Turf Centre. I winced as the flying, blood stained lump churned up what was intended to be the London 2012 shot put field! He limped about and stood looking into the distance, wired to the moon. How the bloody hell was I going to get him home now? I called a vet and they found me a professional transporter who, ever so coolly loaded him onto a 3.5t lorry and safely got us home.

For days I couldn't face handling him, it took every ounce of my being to even check he had everything he needed. I felt emotionally wrecked. This was supposed to be exciting, that 'getting to know you' week was stained with blood and tears. I had to find some light from somewhere, but where? Lord only knew!

ONE STEP FORWARD… 6 STEPS BACK

Months of rehabilitation, the purchase of a big ancient 7.5t horse lorry and some serious soul searching ensued. I gave his wounds time to heal and started long reining♥ and lunging♥ to get some strength into his weak muscles. My first ride was just the same as I had that first day of trying him; slow, unbalanced and VERY wobbly. 8 months passed and we were given the all clear by vet and physio to resume 'business as usual'. I jumped a few cross poles and started hacking♥ a bit with friends, that's when it became very clear that our trust issues were much more deep rooted than the injuries sustained in the accident.

Hacking♥ was a huge issue for us, in the arena♥ he was willing to learn and be educated, out in a field, on a bridle path or the lanes; he scared me. Whilst his external injuries healed, my confidence was a deep open wound. The sweet, young horse, should have had guidance, boundaries, everything I knew I had to give him, but somehow managed to fail at. He needed showing that it was okay, I didn't believe that it was myself so I couldn't tell him that! The experience I had from riding anything I could get my grubby, child size mitts for all of those years that led up to this were lost. All of those 'lost causes' that I had helped train and compete for years, where was that experience now? I had ridden so many breakers♥, youngsters and project horses, I knew the drill. I knew what was required, I just couldn't supply it to poor Freckles and I didn't know why. Those 'Over Horsing' alarm bells that I had seen so often in other people were sounding in my head…

Ring A Ding 1 - Doubting yourself

I began doubting whether I had the capabilities to help him develop and progress. Maybe the problems in my home life were to blame, maybe a combination of things but I was a trembling mess in all areas of my life.

Doubting yourself when dealing with horses, especially young horses that need defined instruction, is only ever going to end in confusion.

Alarm Bell 2 – 'Ding – Dong' there it is … Confusion

Rearing, napping, bolting♥, his way of telling me he was confused. Every time I attempted to leave the yard it ended in tears. I was in way too deep now and every inch of confidence was draining from my trembling body. 8 months passed; I wasn't sure I knew what I was doing anymore. Maybe I should get a hamster, might be safer.

Alarm Bell 3 – Outside influencers

The imaginary pressure from people around me wasn't helping and I felt required to take the lump cross country schooling to prove I still had 'it'. The biggest bell of all…The pressure of external influencers; you do stupid things to prove you're not a giant sack of rotting fruit.

The day started badly because he still wasn't overly confident in loading onto the lorry so when we pulled up to the course I was utterly white with fear. I rode around for a while (just re-living this makes my palms sweat) and decided to attempt a small log. We scrambled over a few tiny jumps but I was having no fun at all. I wanted to cry. Until the point where he simply had had enough, he threw in the towel, shut his eyes and bolted♥. I tried everything to pull him up, he ran through two lines of stock fencing and I bailed out into a hedge. No surprises that we parted company, it was a stupid thing to have taken him before he was ready. But that day, shattered, beaten and terrified - I waved the white flag.

Alarm Bell 4 - Sweating palms? Racing heart? Making excuses not to ride?

If I have learnt one thing (and most certainly the hard way), it's that perseverance isn't always the right path to tread – know when enough is enough, you'll be thankful in the end. Safe to say, I was broken inside, I had persevered for far too long. That day cross country schooling, he ran blind across a field and I had to bail out before I wet my knickers (or worse) – that day was the end of the road for me.

I got home that afternoon to my bloody awful and at that point, frequently venomous marriage and locked myself away. Dragging my knees up to my chin, I sobbed long and hard. How could I have let this happen to me? How could I be sat here broken and unrecognisable? I was barely a shadow of that fun, giggling girl that loved life so much, I felt in mourning for what I had lost. Something had to change, something huge, looking back now I can almost guarantee that I was suffering with severe depression. I would never have admitted it at the time, but I was in a very bad place, one I wanted to run from and never look back. It was dark where I was and I had very few people to tell my worries to, alone again.

3 weeks later I advertised and sold my big grey lump, the very first viewer was a professional dressage♥ rider looking for her next horse to move up the levels. I was honest about my fears and his inexperience. She was kind, didn't seem to mind me blubbering, and made me an offer. I did love Freckles, I loved him but I knew it was the right decision and I so desperately wanted to release myself from the guilt of owning a horse I was terrified of. A week later he passed the vetting♥ and left. I sobbed once more as the

door closed on this chapter of my life. I felt nothing but a let-down, I knew what everyone at the yard must have thought; 'stupid girl, trying to be something she's not'. They were right, I wasn't that person anymore.

So here I was, mentally drained and nothing to show for my sorry start to horse ownership other than bruises and tear stained cheeks, no rosettes♥ or smiling photos of me at shows, it hadn't been fun at all. Enough was enough, I wasn't going down without a fight, ONE LAST TRY. I booked to go and view one of the Queens old show horses, a nine year old, been there and done it, gentleman type. Taking the advice of my new friends and not buying the first one I saw; I sat scrolling through a mountain of adverts only to find one right on my door step. Too convenient to pass up, I went to see the little bay pony first before setting off for the royal visit. He was another young one, but 5 and a nice Master Imp♥ bred horse that seemed to have a nice-ish face.

I turned up to the yard and the little tiny scrawny nugget just stood there looking at me, shoes nearly hanging off, a little sad and poor but sweet and very polite. He had come in to a very reputable breeder to be sold as a favour, not their usual line of business so he was going for little money. I watched a young lad ride him over jumps and I began to sweat and tremble. I couldn't do it, I couldn't get on. Better to find out just down the road I suppose, than drive 200 miles only to poo my pants trying the other one!! I was coaxed into mounting and he really was a saint, I was tense and quivering and this little angel carried me around without any fuss. I went into trot and then canter, suddenly regaining that glimmer of what I used to know. I popped a small cross pole and I felt wonderful. I found something that minute, that split second, something that had been missing for years. I approached a bloody great oxer♥, easily 90cms; he soared it, we were flying, I was flying. I cried tears of relief and ecstasy for the first time in years. I didn't want to get off, I loved him for restoring my faith that day, so I paid the lady, cancelled the royal viewing and hacked him home. Pauldarys Master Patrick, Pat to his mates – made me VERY happy from day one.

This little horse was the most wonderful thing that could have ever happened to me back then. I had mentally detached myself from my abusive marriage and within 3 months I was confident enough to join a riding club♥ and do some local dressage♥ shows. Pat would get a rosette♥ every single time we went out, I smiled every second I was sat on this horse, he really did (and still does) make my heart sing. We made so many wonderful friends through the riding club and for two and a half blissful years, we were just perfect for each other. We competed in dressage regionally and nationally, piles of rosettes and trophies were accumulating and I was so in love, nothing else mattered in the world. You can just bloody well guarantee that when one part of your life is just plain perfect, another part falls apart around your ears.

REVERTING

Now, this was the part that was meant to say '…and they all lived happily ever after'. Not bloody likely! My husband was posted another 65 miles west of what was already far enough and because my job was becoming more of a career instead of a time filler, I decided to rent Monday to Friday with friends. A string of violent arguments meant I was actually glad to see the back of him for those days too. I grew independent and loved every second of being my own person away from a suffocating marriage. It also meant that I had absolutely no money. I rode horses for other people before and after work and got a weekend job to pay my rent and keep Pat but it wasn't enough. I was exhausted, Pat always got left until last and I felt cr*p again. I was forever putting fuel and food on credit cards and was slowly sinking further and further into debt. Something had to give.

I remember the day I wrote the advert, not a 'for sale' one but just as bad – Horse for Loan. I cried and cried over how I could possibly explain to another person just how much this horse meant to me. I wanted to find him a temporary home until I got enough experience to progress in my marketing career to warrant a promotion and pay increase. It might be a year, it might even be two, but it killed me all the same. Pat was my life, his shaggy Irish mane had soaked up more tears than I care to remember, how would I cope without him? Turns out, word of mouth found him a very nice lady who would let me come and see him as often as I wanted, she was local and it was the best of a bad situation. Pat an I had a glorious time at the Riding Club National Championships and he left for his new home the following weekend. It was lonely without him, I started doing stupid things like jogging to fill the gap. I kept on with the three jobs and squirreled away all the money I could to pay back my debt.

In December, I called time on my marriage, it had been over for at least a year and this was closure. I had become independent, I didn't need controlling anymore and I didn't need to feel constantly depressed about what should have been wonderful. Today, I feel absolutely no negativity towards my first husband. I feel nothing but educated. I have learnt so much about myself because of that period in time and no one can ever take that from me. The worst thing, something that very nearly tipped my life over the edge once more, was not leaving behind my marriage but leaving behind my three fur babies. Those with animals will understand just how much they mean to you and how they can wrench you heart out of your chest when you least expected. I had 3 cats; Fatsy Kensit, Stinky Fish and Little Man who had been there for me just like Pat had for years. I sobbed my eyes out all the way home leaving them behind and every night after that for months. I would visit at weekends and stay in the army house with them, like a visiting order in a prison, I'm not sure it made things better or worse but I knew it wasn't forever.

NOW WHAT?!

A blissful Christmas came, I was so happy to be free of my old life. I was a new person and I was finding myself at last. Right when I least expected it I fell in love. Yep, you heard right!! I realised right there and then that it was probably the first time too. I was totally head over heels in love and nothing, I mean nothing could bring me down. It was 'the chap from work' who, in our house, we had named "Gary the Arrogant Arse". He was so obnoxious and rude to everyone, but dig deeper and he was so wonderfully kind and my Lord, did I want to take his clothes off. He wore just a little too tight trousers that I used to gawp across at every time he left the room. I just wanted to kiss his hairy hand every time he gave me a document or helped me with my work, Christ what was wrong with me?! My heart raced just getting dressed in the mornings, I felt giggly and was desperate to be left in a room alone with this poor bloke.

Now, Gary is VERY switched on and whilst I uncontrollably threw myself at him on more than one occasion, he remained aloof, casual and ever so cool. It made me want him MORE. I was relentless in my obvious affection and made advances that couldn't have gone unnoticed. My skirts got slightly shorter, I wore stockings instead of tights and I took every opportunity to make this combination clearly visible by retrieving things that I casually dropped near his desk. Oh the shame! But I was smitten, I wasn't giving up and apparently all my morals had been left at home along with my tights.

It was December, I had handed in my notice (mainly because Gary the Arrogant Arse had told me that he wouldn't want to cavort with anyone from the office) and that fateful day finally arrived. The acceptance of my after-work-drinks invitation. I sh*t myself, I won't lie and I was terrified about what we would actually talk about when we were in a pub, alone. How would I stop myself just leaning over and licking his beard? Bugger it, we got on great actually and conversation was fine, although I did laugh nervously a lot. But then it happened, he walked me to my car and kissed me, so expertly and for such a long time, I felt my knees buckle. With his arm around my back, pulling in my trembling body, I felt like I was in the final scene of Bridget Jones' Diary, snogging the face off Colin Firth! BLOODY WOWZERS... for the drive home and the whole of that weekend, I was on the biggest high of my life!!! I didn't get off this high for weeks.

The first time I 'slept over' was a few weeks on, we attended a pub quiz with his mates and the plan was not to go home... I was so terribly nervous about being cr*p in bed that I drank FAR too much wine, made a dick of myself at the quiz and didn't really remember much of the bedroom bit anyway! Once that was out of the way, we were very quickly one of those annoying couples, sickeningly in love and totally oblivious of anyone else. Most days, even now, I still feel like that too.

In just 2 months, we rented a house together. Quick to most people, but I knew living with someone was make or break, luckily this 'made' us. It also meant that I could get my three cat babies back with me, one of the happiest days of my life. Gary was greeted by three furry hooligans who on the first meeting, Stinky Fish vomited her newly eaten biscuits all over the floor and like always, Fatsy Kensit came in and took pleasure in gobbling up the pre-chewed lumps – Gary laughed (Thank Christ)!! In February, the phone rang. A fresh chilly morning and a bit too much nice pony food and Pat had launched his temporary mother into orbit and frightened her. It was late February when he came home, only 6 months into our year long agreement. I was secretly delighted – not for her injuries but because my boy was coming home, I had a better job, a man who supported my love for this horse and I was so happy, it was all falling into place.

A BAD DAY ACTUALLY

It was Saturday morning, I remember it like it was just last week. I watched the trailer pull up the drive, so desperately excited to introduce Gary to the other love of my life, very child-like in my emotions, I was squeaking with joy as he bumped down the track. We unloaded him and let him off the headcollar into the arena. He lifted his tail, bucked♥ and farted; Gary laughed. We watched him prance and snort for a few minutes before I decided I wanted to get on. I wanted to ride my wonderful boy, my old comfy arm chair again. I saddled him up whilst Gary fed him carrots, I led him to the mounting block and hopped on. He felt incredible, just like always. The pride was bursting out of my skin, Gary was filming from the edge of the arena. Now I don't really know what happened next. It was all a bit hazy but it changed my life again. That split second, the decision to ride, the day, the time; it changed EVERYTHING.

I think my stirrup knocked the fence or something startled him in the trees because in a split second, my darling horse, my rock steady boy was doing the best rendition of a rodeo bull the world had ever seen! He jinked and spun, head between his knees. I was launched into orbit before I had time to think about how to handle the explosion and landed on my head on the foot of a wooden jump stand. Massively concussed I stood up and found my very wayward bearings. I HAD to get back on, I was always taught that, even if you get on and walk two steps- it was enough. I got back on, shaking like a dog having a sh*t. I walked a circle and got off. All of those awful feelings came flooding back, the sweating, the tears, the tightness in my chest, it was all there just how it was before. I cried for days on and off. I cannot tell you what this did to me, how it reverted me back to the days of wishing the ground would swallow me whole. I couldn't shake it off, I thought it would be temporary – it wasn't.

For 5 months I didn't ride him. I turned him away in a field, let him forget about that day and got him thoroughly checked over. Physiotherapist, vet, chiropractor, farrier, horse whisperer you name it, I tried it. I was absolutely terrified of riding him. I couldn't face it at all. I was lucky to have been given another horse to ride alongside him, this got my confidence back but just made the guilt of it not being Pat even worse.

Little Pea was a lovely dark brown thoroughbred mare just 15.2hh but a heart as big as a lions. She was with me so that I could produce her to be sold for her wonderful owner. She was safe and loyal and we fell in love too but Pat was the one breaking my heart. Pea and I went everywhere together, we jumped jumps and hacked and did everything that I so wanted to do with Pat, that I used to do with him. I led him out on rides from Pea and very occasionally plucked up the courage to get on him, never for more than ten minutes and always just in walk.

Now, during this time, Daddy Carrot (Gary's new 'Pat' name) had proposed to me. It was the absolute best timing, I was feeling low and there is nothing that could have made me happier than to agree to marry the man I adored. He had spent all day laying out rose petals and lighting hundreds of candles and presented me with the most beautiful pink sapphire engagement ring in the most romantic hotel room you could possibly imagine. He knew me so well, that touched me more than any of it. I was in heaven. We bought wedding magazines and set a date; 9th July 2016.

MOVING ON (AND ON)!

October 2015 we moved homes and subsequently moved livery♥ yards and I was then very vulnerable in a big place where everyone was a bit of a 'doer'. Little Pea went off to her new home and I was left with the pressure of Pat and I alone again, like a nervous first date! Most of the other people on the yard couldn't really understand why I had a horse that I never rode and that was perfectly sound. I found myself feeling pressured and a bit bullied – all in my head I'm sure, but this made things much worse. I would get to the yard at 5am just to avoid judgemental eyes, I was paying livery money for the pleasure of being thoroughly ashamed of my fear. I think for the second time in my life, I was depressed. Fear is a violent thing if you try to conceal it, it will destroy you from the inside and despite how good an actress I had become over the years, I was crumbling once more. My relationship with Gary was suffering too, I was sad quite often and this made him worry, I could just tell things weren't ok.

I cried most nights after coming back from the yard, a few times I lied about having a lovely ride only to have sat in my car watching the birds and just changing into my jodhpurs before I left. Denial and fear were consuming my life but the truth is - I couldn't ride, I trembled every time I got his tack♥ out. Driving from work to the stables I could barely grip the steering wheel through sweating palms, eyes stinging with tears through the total fear of having to ride him. I was so scared. I remember planning a secret ride on a cold morning in February. I didn't want anyone knowing for fear of spectators. I had taken his hind shoes taken off by then to save money thinking I would turn him away in a field again or keep him as a pet. I got on and walked up the path to the arena, it was a little bit frosty and I could see my breath but I wasn't cold. I was violently trembling and sweat was running down my forehead and into my eyes. I walked a circle and struggled to get my breath. The dizziness was so bad and not being able to breathe, I quickly got off, ran to the arena fence and vomited. I spewed bile because knowing I was going to ride I hadn't eaten for 12 hours. This wasn't fun anymore, it was making me ill. I sobbed into his shaggy un-pulled mane, why did I feel like this? Through the tears I explained to him that I loved him but it was over for us, he had to have a new mummy now but I would make sure she was nice, crikey did I sob (I am now just reliving it). At this dark stage of my tunnel there really was no other way out of my grief and guilt than to sell him, I didn't know which of these things broke my heart the most.

In April 2016 I made a call to a professional event horse producer, talked through the costs, the process and what it involved to sell my horse. I cried twice on the phone to this poor woman. I was at my wits end, fear spiralling out of control but finding it equally as hard to let go of something I loved more than life itself. This was the darkest place I had been for years, animals consume you if you let them – a third world problem it may seem, but this was a tribulation of pure love not financial gain. I loved this horse more than life but the guilt and fear were eating me alive. I remember sitting in my car with tears rolling down my cheeks, it was raining, I just looked through the window at his face in the barn and he whickered to me. It was probably for food but I doubted myself for making the call and arrangements that were taking shape. I got home and I will never forget it as long as I live, that question Daddy Carrot put to me as I explained what I had done.

Very calmly, my soon to be Husband looked me in the eyes and said, "Will you regret this for the rest of your life?" – It was instant, the answer was undoubtedly "yes". He followed it with; "Imagine how you will feel watching someone out having fun with him, smiling and loving him and winning just like you should be, just like you did before." That was it. That was my motivation. Right there. In that moment, I was NOT going to let someone else love

MY horse, I loved him, no-one else. I called off the sales arrangements and decided to deal with whatever it was after the wedding. Lord knows I needed a sunny break more than I realised!

THE I DO'S

In the run up to our wedding day it had become apparent that, whilst I had been so consumed in my own equine related misery I had failed to print invitations, do table plans or lose enough weight to fit into my dress. At the end of May, 6 weeks before the wedding date, I sent out invitations, borrowed my parents treadmill and began planning our wedding. We had budgeted £4000 for the entire event including honeymoon and in West Sussex this was tough – but not impossible. I literally made EVERYTHING myself at home. My dress was £100 from eBay. I bought a size 8 hoping I would squeeze into it by the time the day arrived… FAT CHANCE I am and always will be on the chubbier side of a size 10! With a few alterations we made it fit and it is the most priceless piece of clothing I will ever own. It had a massive, princess style full skirt, fitted lace bodice and beautiful lace straps on the shoulders. I stitched a wide pink satin ribbon around the middle and it was simply unique, a one off, much like its wearer!

With the help of some much loved friends and family, the day was nothing but magical. We had a small church ceremony followed by a village hall reception. We did a funny quiz after our fish and chip supper and our guests enjoyed a good hour of my murderous singing on the karaoke. I couldn't have been happier to have married my best friend, my Daddy Carrot; it was perfect.

On the Monday we flew to the Caribbean and by day 4, I had had just about enough of too much food, too much booze and too much sun. It appears that I am cr*p at holidaying, I missed the cats and Pat terribly and as a distraction I began re-inventing myself.

Day 6 of honeymoon bliss, I had a monumental psychological breakthrough. Picture this: laying on a massage table, nothing but the sound of the air-conditioning unit whirring and my new husband breathing all too loudly on the bed next to me; I had a revelation. I began a thought process that put me in the XC start box♥, being counted down and feeling the elation of having got through the dressage without leaving the boards and round the swim of coloured jumps without jabbing my horse in the chops too many times. I was there, just like I used to be – EXCITED, not scared, not vomiting, no stains in my under garments. Long story short, away from reality I was totally and utterly ready for it! Could I really feel like this in the flesh, could I go through with it? There was only one way to find out!

We came back to the UK Saturday morning after a dog of an overnight flight and tried to remain positive. I asked Daddy Carrot to come and get some video of me sailing over some terrifyingly big jumps, but tiredness took over. Queue the excuses… the poor pony, having had 2 weeks off getting fat would surely die of shock if all of a sudden, I decided to become Mrs Mary King♥ whilst on holiday – We'll leave it for one night in the week and lunge the poor sod instead, URGH… I was already losing the inner strength that I had found on that massage table.

Instead, for the first time in years I clicked that over anticipated link on the British Eventing website – FIXTURES, and chose my fate. If I planned and paid for an event that I couldn't really afford post wedding, I would feel immense guilt about bailing out! I was reluctant to say it out loud, like the date of your driving test in case you over egg it and let everyone down, but there it was - entered…. Littleton Manor Equestrian Centre 8th October. It gave me exactly 74 days, 11 hours and (as of that terrifying moment) 45 minutes to not die choking on my own vomit or of starvation unable to eat for fear!

BISH BASH BOSH!

The week we got home from honeymoon paradise I moved Pat again, to a much more laid back place. A small yard where no-one knew me, where I could be anything or anyone I wanted without the pre-requisite of reputation. I decided I wasn't going to be scared and that I was going to look like I knew what I was doing and so I arrived an event rider.

Now, people will judge you for near on anything in the equestrian world but there is no real right or wrong beyond the basic needs of your horse. So judge away, but for 2 whole weeks, I gave him a milligram of Sedalin gel♥ before I rode (in secret, obviously). It made me much less terrified. In the bag with the Sedalin was a hipflask, 3 or 4 gulps of port stopped the very obvious trembling of my limbs and with a steady horse and steady hands and legs I hacked more times in a matter of weeks than I had in the whole time I have owned him. I actually started enjoying it too. As a result, he calmed down to a kickable lump and I felt braver, less nervous and in turn entered a rather civilised sounding 'Champagne Breakfast Ride' with my local hunt.

The fateful Saturday arrived, I frequented the loo 4 times before I left the house, I had hardly eaten for 2 days out of nervousness but it appeared my bowels hadn't got the memo! With my uneaten toast left on the kitchen side I was trembling lighting a cigarette as I got into the car for what could be the last drive of my life! Fully expecting to be carted off in a body bag that day, I made a note of my friend Suzi's phone number and left it on the dash board. Suzi and I have always agreed that she would have Pat if anything happened to me, I felt like it might have been necessary for me to leave the number available that day!!

I got to the yard (pretended to be brave), tacked up and hacked the 1.5 mile path to what felt like my untimely death. He stood at the meet with 70 other horses and was WELL ready to go when they finally trotted off, I waved my ever-supportive Daddy Carrot off and there I was; a lamb to the slaughter! The first section was a long gallop up a steep hill which massively helped my nerves. I had no brakes but, by the top of the hill, you didn't need them. All of the horses were slowing from tired legs. Thank goodness!

I kept him at the front of the ride as the pace was pretty fast throughout and slippery footing meant I wanted a good run at the JUMPS – YES...THERE WERE JUMPS!!!. I clutched the neck strap over tiger traps and logs, we soared over ditches and galloped with no brakes – I felt BLOODY FANTASTIC. For the first time in over 5 years I felt like I was invincible again. I was my 15 year old self out hunting and absolutely loving it. I hacked home after two hours of life changing riding. I screamed at the top of my lungs in the middle of an open field, the release from that shell of fear, the shell had cracked, I was like a chick breaking his egg...not quite flying yet but my goodness, there was some huge potential ahead!

I'm literally sobbing with pride, covered in goose bumps writing this out – I never thought I would ever do anything like that ever again! I was on cloud 9 for over a week; I felt capable and as though I could actually do this, I could ACTUALLY be an event rider again.

Photos by LRG Photography

Photo by LRG Photography

#wimpyeventer

In September 2016, I felt that I had tormented my husband with tails of my pony woes for too long. I was desperate not to be one of those wives that talked all day and night about their horses to a long suffering, non-horsey husband.

I thought I would set up a Facebook page and website to document my tales and with that; Diary of a Wimpy Eventer was born. Originally a page to outline my fears, progress and boost my confidence, who knew that today I would have a following of over 13,000 people and have achieved so much more than the original plan.

Throughout the last 10 years of my marketing career I have grasped a good handle on how to promote other people and their businesses, what a different kettle of fish it is promoting yourself!! I am so proud of how much this page helps others that are swimming against the same tide, you deserve to feel that shell breaking feeling, that dark into light that I have felt – I want to help you feel that.

So here we are – right from the start, as raw and as real as ever, documented from one Imodium fuelled experience to another. Enjoy!

September 2016

13th September 2016

Give me a hand out of this hole will you?!

So, a bit of a sorry state of affairs after my run of cast iron balls activities. First off, I was massively on the up after my 'mock hunting' experience at the Champagne breakfast ride, so thought this would make day to day riding, clinics ♥ and popping a small fence in the school a doddle. With the right mind set, I entered for a show jumping ♥ clinic at Brinsbury College and when asked what height I wanted to jump – very boldly wrote back 90 cms!!! WTF was I thinking (scuse' the language). I know this might not seem a huge feat to most of you, but when Daddy Carrot put a 70 cm jump up in the arena to practice over for the big day – I just wanted to get off. I almost cried and almost certainly had a change of undies looming.

Saturday morning came and I was literally white as a sheet walking down the field to retrieve my poor horse! I gave him a small calmer syringe ♥ (Lord knows why I didn't syringe it, and the rest of the pack of 3 straight into my own mouth!). I got all my gear on – jumping saddle (borrowed from a friend), branded jacket (from days gone by when I didn't tremble so often) and my new INVINCIBILITY BOOTS** donated out of support and kindness by a fabulous company that I think took pity on my tale of woes. We certainly looked the business!! On arrival I was delighted to see the jumps were tiny and the 2 people in the group before me were hitting the deck and getting up laughing! PHEW!

We went in, perfect dressage moves across the arena, medium trot ♥, counter canter *SHOW OFF ALERT* but then I remembered why we had come and my heart sank. We began over a cross pole that my cats could have jumped over, clinging onto the neck strap ♥ with white knuckles – breathing a sigh of relief over not dying, I jumped a few single fences before being picked out of the group as the first course jumper. Well… they were 85cms, I didn't faint, I didn't cry, I kept a nice rhythm, put my leg on where I needed to and got each jump foot perfect. I literally couldn't have been happier – jumped the course once more in the session and because of how thrilled I was to be alive, I decided to quit while I was ahead!!

I hacked home with a grin on my face as the tension pains in my chest subsided, another happy outing doing something out of my comfort zone! Next weekend is DRESSAGE. A competition environment where I feel a little more confident in our capabilities. We have two competition days in a row – day one is two Novice tests and day two is a Novice and Elementary! I have also found a chum to buddy up with at a HUNTER TRIAL♥ on 2nd Oct and I absolutely MUST get Cross Country schooling♥ at Littleton before the fateful BE day! Please hold my hand!!

**INVINCIBILITY BOOTS – The box arrived and the first word I read on it was Cognac…I thought my luck was changing and they came with a free bottle. Alas, it was the colour – I have been through pairs of death boots before and these looked not all that dissimilar. BUT…they haven't once made my feet pound with circulation loss. I feel invincible in them – I put one foot in, zipped them up and it was like someone had melted them to my legs – they are grippy, elegant and described as "the perfect choice for any top-level rider." WELL THAT'S ALL RIGHT THEN!!!!!

16th September 2016

I've only gone and done it!!!

Well that's is… My feet are wet, I've jumped in with them both! – My. Entry. Has. Been. Accepted!!!

In actual fact, it's not my feet that are wet, it's my palms and my forehead, I'm sat at my desk looking at last year's course photos, already choosing the one I might die at. With any luck I'll get balloted anyway as there are 126 in the class!!

Jumping session tonight before our clinic tomorrow, might brave something bigger than a 1ft.6 cross pole, I've got spare pants in the car!

19th September 2016

I'm pretty p*ssed off that I cannot remember which pants I was wearing on Friday night when Daddy Carrot made his largest erection to date...

We flew a jump at 110 cms and I actually remained stain less... Whatever was I thinking!

Now, as I have a following of nearly 400 people (thank you all for your support) I thought I would like to introduce to you, my lovely boy; here is his 'Pony Profile'.

Name- Pauldarys Master Patrick

Sire - Master Imp

Stable Name - Pat

Colour - Bay (Orange with black long bits - mane, tail, legs, ears!)

Age - 10

Favourite Activities - Spooking♥ at birds, spooking at bags, spooking at leaves, stealing food.

Pats Story - Born and broken in Ireland, brought to Hampshire by the lovely people at Pauldarys stud. Bought by myself in June 2012.

Since then we have competed for riding club teams, been to the British Riding Club National Championships, been hunting, cross country schooling, hacked to the pub, reached elementary dressage wins, British Novice jumping and this weekend we embark on our first ever BE.

He is my best friend in the whole wide world.

26th September 2016

Gin and Tramadol…. A cocktail of success!!!

What a weekend!! Let's start from Wednesday night where the plans to run through my Novice and Elementary♥ tests for Sunday were scheduled. I left the office, grabbed my breeches from the car and strolled over to get changed. One leg in, two legs in, yank on the too tight breeches… TWANG!!!! My lower back left me in a crumpled, screaming heap on the toilet floor. An hour on the Tens machine and a glass of wine from super nice yard owners and I was on the horse – only able to walk.

Drat and blast… I had entered two bloody shows and paid upfront for them for this weekend!! I wasn't even the slightest bit relieved that I might have a 'get out of jail free card'. I rested, tens machined and iced it for 2 days, the more I moved about, the better it got – enough to run through the tests on Friday night but sadly, no jump practice ready for Saturday!

The day dawned, I had my times for the 80 and 90 cm classes and I wasn't set to face my doom until 3.30 pm… *all day to worry about it… Bloody Marvellous*. I was SICK to my stomach with nerves, literally. I took two Imodium caplets, a tramadol and bought two Gin and Tonic ready mixed cans from the garage which I downed one on the way to the yard whilst chuffing half a packet of cigarettes!!

I arrived and the nerves were still leaving me utterly hopeless. I couldn't remember the course at all, I watched about 20 other horses go round and it WAS NOT HELPING! I heard the gate lady shouting my number, ARSE BAGS.... Kick, kick off we go... As if by some wondrous miracle, I made it over the first 6 fences clear and into the timed area which I went no quicker for!! I just went for the steady clear, mainly based on the fact that, any quicker and I would have been sick!

I had an unfortunate pole and a very steady time but I DID IT!!!!! Totally elated I very nearly quit whilst I was ahead and cancelled the 90cm entry but it started quick smart and I felt pressured into 'manning up'. Well, would you believe it ... I only bloody did that one as well!!! Another silly pole down where I got in a bit close but we bloody did it, we jumped the biggest course we had done in 10 years, with a dodgy back and blurred gin goggles on!!! WOOOHOOOOOOOOOOO!!!!!! I hacked home with the biggest grin and the biggest hangover forming!!

SUNDAY FUNDAY...I was MUCH less worried about the dressage on Sunday. Way more in our comfort zone, so I will keep it brief... I went in winging it slightly after a short warm up and not really knowing the tests but he was soft, rideable and fitting an elementary into a 20x40 wasn't nearly as bum squeaky as I thought - so here goes nothing - I ONLY BLOODY WON BOTH CLASSES! I hit a 72 percent in the novice with 9s for the free walk and 67 percent in the Elementary even with a 4.5 for an egg shaped circle and an error of course ;)   I literally couldn't be happier – The best weekend we have had in a very long time!!! I think my shrivelled up balls are inflating a little!

October 2016

11th October 2016

So with reinvention going swimmingly, I am about to grace you with the first affiliated competition report that I have EVER done. I have read thousands of them written by brave riders and I never imagined I would be writing my own. I will add, although I am writing this report, I am nowhere near a brave rider, I am an excellent actress and kidding myself into think this sport of Eventing is a good idea. – I am still 95% terrified 2% determined and 3% in too deep and can't turn back!!

I cannot believe what I am about to write – I'll take you back to Friday night....

Daddy Carrot and I went over to Littleton Manor Equestrian Centre to walk the vomit inducing XC course at approximately 6.37pm. We arrived, found the start, smoked a cigarette and by fence 13 – it was PITCH BLOODY BLACK!! I was having a mini (internal) meltdown whilst remaining silently cool on the exterior for the purpose of appearing nonchalant about the whole thing.

Dinner and bed (an early night... not the norm on what has been named 'Pub Friday' in our usual weekly schedule). I slept surprisingly well, woke up not too terrified but I was buggered if I could remember ANY of the jumps past number 2!! – Ah well, I can remember my dressage test – that's a 3rd of the way down my poorly lit BE road!!!

Having plaited the night before, I re-tapped Pats stud holes and got him ready for the off, crikey I needed a poo. We arrived in lots of time, I visited the toilet a few times, smoked a few cigarettes and desperately tried to strap my spurs on through trembling hands and legs!! Having mounted WAY too early, I bobbled about a bit getting used to riding on grass in an outline – Piss poor planning etc.... I hadn't ridden in an outline on grass for about 3 years!

Into the test, it was *fine*, no more, no less. I did everything where I should do it but having scored nearly 75% at Novice and Elementary this year, I was annoyed that I hadn't devoted more time to improving our skills of 'field dressage' – 33.6 percent - Meh… neither happy nor sad over this – I know where I need to improve so I'm trying not to punish myself too much!

25 minutes later, I was 4 holes shorter in the stirrup and flying a couple of practice jumps, pretty much ready to go into the show jumping – so I did!! I think the more time you dwell on the prospect of jumping your round, the more likely you are to get nervous and f*ck it up… do not linger about like a wet fart in the warm up – 3 practice jumps is enough to not put the willies up us, but enough to have stretched out any post dressage tension. Surprisingly, I remembered where I was going, didn't fluff too much with him and left him dis-united in one corner instead of tampering with the rhythm – wrong or right – it got us round CLEAR♥!!! I ACTUALLY COULDN'T BELIEVE IT!!!!!

Now onto my doom…

I was TERRIFIED, I mean literally on the verge of tears. My first cross country round in forever. I had looked at the course pictures and had a pretty good idea of the route but it wasn't helping my fragile confidence. Just re-living this now is making me need a poo! I got him ready with the help of my trusty pal and escort for the day while trying to have a bite of banana – NO CHANCE… queue the first gag reflex!!!

Down at the warm up I put my number down and jumped 3 practice jumps (worked for us in the show jumping, not lingering/wet fart/bla bla bla!!) and just walked around trying not to spew bile all over his mane. The straps of my body protector forcing the vomit into my throat; I wasn't at all ready to go. "Number 123, can you make your way to the start please?" F*cking NO, no I cannot!! I want to go home now please, I do not want to be here of jump any of those bloody jumps, thank you.

The countdown of a minute felt like an eternity, I explained to the counter downer that I wanted to get off and go home now please, she wished me luck – That was it... 5,4,3,2,1...crack, crack of the whip on my poor horses arse (mainly for my benefit) and we were FLYING...

Every stride down to the first fence felt AMAZING, we were galloping, flying and soared over the first fence – it was the best bloody feeling in the whole world – adrenalin just completely took over. The second jump, a row of HAYGAIN steamers, I was worried about him looking them at so one more bum smack and he flew it... I felt as though 3, 4, 5, 6 and 7 – the steps, flew by without blinking, he backs off but if I'm there kicking his arse, he will go. 8 (the corner) I was worried about, no need – he was bloody flying. The horse that cross country schooled like a 4 year old only a fortnight before, felt like an absolute machine – I screamed "Good Boy!" and "YIP YIP!" at the top of my lungs before and after every fence!!!

Nothing was a problem for this horse today, nothing – we flew down the home straight over 15, 16 and finally 17 – I let out the biggest wail of joy you have ever heard and then through my horrendous unfit heavy breathing, cried like a baby!!! I dived off and undid everything – NEVER in my life have I felt love for an animal like I did right at that moment. (Christ, I'm now at my desk in a communal office – CRYING!! SH*T SH*T SH*T!!!) My horse and me; we were doing it – actually achieving what we set out to in tremendous style.

Back at the box, pony sorted, Daddy Carrot and top buddy came running over – I was currently in 3rd place!!! Bloody 3rd place!!!!!!! I didn't want him standing on the box all day so we decided to take him home and I would come back for the score draws.

Driving back, convincing myself that the rest of the section would have overtaken me by now – I was ridiculously delighted to see ***5th*** by our names!!! We came 5th…. Our first EVER one day event, affiliated♥ too – I was beaming – donning 2 rosettes and a great bag of prizes, I drove home – Couldn't resist going back to the yard to tell Pat how amazing he was and give him an extra carrot.

We are 3 days on now and I still feel on top of the world, pride and happiness over what we achieved – what I have achieved is just so overwhelming. I overcame some SERIOUS anxiety to even fill out the entry form, let alone give it everything we had on the day. I just want to say a remarkably HUGE thank you to everyone that has offered words of support, well-wishers, wine bringers, to my long suffering husband and team of friends for listening to my woes and mostly, thank you to my horse – he is, after all, the best thing I have ever encountered in the world EVER.

Who says the horse world is full of back stabbing, interfering arsebags?! For every wrong un' you've all proved there's a lovely, kind hearted and truly fabulous goodun'.

Thank you all. 😊 😊 🖤 🖤

20th October 2016

Let me explain a few things now I'm older and more wisdom-ous?!

I am pretty sure that at some point in the lives of every single one of you reading this, you have felt rotten about your capabilities, downtrodden or had your chips totally p*ssed on by someone else. If you haven't – you are probably the one doing the urinating!

My equestrian side of life has been FULL to the bloody handle with highs and lows of the best and worst kind. Along the way, you realise the people that you surround yourself with are those that influence the success or failure. From my experience the pride or guilt you feel for winning and the shame or experience you get from ballsing it up, is all determined by the first 3 people you tell.

My choice of 3 include; No.1 – My husband; he almost always congratulates me on survival before any results are divulged. I am reminded that I do this for enjoyment and like we always say, the minute you stop enjoying the ride, get off the bus. No.2 – Fellow yard people; which I am delighted to say – couldn't give two sh*ts if I succeed or fail, they are just happy peering in from the edge at someone having a bash at it! There is no hidden agenda behind their "Ooo you're alive then, how did you get on?" No.3 – My social media 'family'; I enjoy how even the non-horsey brigade give me a 'wow' like! (What is the world coming to?!)

This hasn't always been the case and I won't ever dwell on that feeling of coming home from a show elated to find that Lady Big Knickers has already got her pants down ready to put your fire out. Those sorts of people, Daddy Carrot and I refer to as; Eleven-erife. If you've been to Tenerife… guess where they've been?! Always waiting in the corner to make you feel like cr*p about yourself.

I like to think that I have always been a good sport at dishing out credit where it's due and of course Karma is a wonderful thing but, the basics are very simple; surround yourself with people that either couldn't give a sh*t, ones that would give their last sh*t to see you succeed, or that ones that don't know what sh*t you're doing! It will almost certainly improve your life and boost your confidence.

24ᵗʰ October 2016

Here we are again…

It's like the morning after the night before – Sat at my huge paper covered desk in my lonely office blogging rather than going through my ton of emails. Did I have a good weekend? I think so. Friday, as you may have seen from my Facebook page, I had another 'moment'. My fragile shreds of confidences with set alight and I wobbled. Sometimes it feels as though the boat is still, the sea is calm and we can go forth into the breach… Other times, I feel like the bloody Titanic when it hit that massive iceberg… Or rather like the bloke that jumped onto the propeller as it was sinking!!

On reflection, Friday makes me want to cry, but so did the half dead squirrel on the road this morning and the bloody rancid coffee I had made for me when I got to work… I think I might be coming down with something!! BLOODY GET A SODDING GRIP YOU GREAT BIG FANNY!!!!!!!!!!!

Honestly, sometimes I don't know what gets into me, dwelling on negatives will get you NOWHERE!

So let's focus on the positives - Saturday I decided to get on with it and go to my jumping clinic. I arrived a little early and got on joined by 3 others of varying levels! Sometimes I wonder whether this is the best way for us to learn but if nothing else, it gives my horse the chance to jump in more of a 'warm up' environment that usually scares the living sh*t out of me. We jumped round a little too enthusiastically, which always makes me smile - as the jumps get bigger (90 cms+) he starts to back off a bit which is a welcomed relief for my twitchy bum! We ended the clinic on a high jumping around a decent course and hacked home with a smile on our faces!!

Saturday night we unusually joined in with some village activities, watching the local fireworks display albeit from the pub... Someone (me) might have had a few too many drinks (totally bloody steaming) and didn't make it home until almost 1am, Daddy Carrot much more soberly in tow! Apparently (little that I remember) I was partaking in activities of the more ...ahem... 'horizontal' ... kind until the wee hours!! Honestly – WHAT IS WRONG WITH ME!!! Drinking to excess is NOT something I make a habit of and why do I not do that....? SUNDAY MORNING is why!!!!!!!!!!!! My word, it was like a diseased hamster had crawled into my ear and puked its guts out into my brain. One large fried breakfast and a sleep later and I was tying my stock♥ ready to go jumping!!

Arrived at Coombelands with not many to go before us, I watched 5 or 6 go to get the course learnt and off we went!! He was flying! I wasn't sure whether I was enjoying it too much as I was concentrating so hard on trying not to push for the flier! I always prefer to go off a long stride but it's not always the best thing for my speedy steed! We had an unfortunate rail where I just got it wrong but we were quick enough to hear our names being called out for the placings!! We were 8th amongst a multitude of nippy ponies. RESULT!!

The 90cm course changed somewhat, it introduced us to our first triple bar and after 10 or so riders round the course – we were in! Never mind the triple bar, I rode like a triple amputee – didn't pick him up at all – at one point, it was like time had stood still and I was coming to a big oxer thinking 'he's doing it all by himself – I am literally straddled over the arm of sofa, still drunk!' Bless the cotton socks of my lovely boy, he did nurse us round to have another unfortunate pole – but what a horse – he was giving it everything, jumping me out of the saddle over most of them. He really did try for me and I was actually bursting with pride. Where I selfishly gave him 35 percent effort, he met me with the remaining 65 and saved our bacon. I cannot tell you all how much I love this horse. He is truly the one in a million that I have dreamed of my entire life and he's mine, sod the bloody lottery!!!

Lastly, I want to thank everyone that wished us well on Friday and over the weekend. It means so very much to me that people actually give two hoots, I cannot tell you what a difference it makes. If it wasn't for everyone rooting for me through this ridiculous diary, I would have stayed slumped in a heap on the sofa yesterday – I couldn't face a post of disappointment to all of you that had taken the time to write to me. So, with everything I have left to give…thank you very much indeed. xxx

October 22, 2016

A comment from my dear patient jump trainer today has left me feeling super - "Vic, your confidence from when I first saw you 3 years ago has gone through the roof" Mwhahaha… little does he know how I'm dying on the inside.

The reality is that Diary of a Wimpy Eventer is the best thing that could have happened to my confidence, I have a purpose now – creating a reason to carry on going – no matter what that reason is, is very important indeed. Course walking this evening at Pachesham ready for the hunter trial♥ tomorrow - We are on at 12.42pm if anyone is interested in 'time of death'.

31st October 2016

Champagne fuelled Red Ribbons!

So, with our late entry accepted into the Pachesham Hunter Trial for the 85 cm pairs class, the usual nervous course walk Friday night was a little less toilet trip inducing than other events. I'm not overly sure why. Maybe my fragile confidence is slowly being coated in honey ready for being rolled in feathers but nonetheless, I felt quite 'alright' about most of the fences, the warm up and not dying! I had 3 small glasses of Malbec in the pub afterwards to quash any last minute terror, I think it worked! I woke up Saturday morning feeling like I might well be able to stomach a slice of toast... VERY ODD INDEED!!

Got Pat ready for a 10am pick up from my trusted sidekick for the day. Let me introduce to you my lovely friend and unofficial confidence coach, Lisa – She and her lovely little mare have been dragged to many an event in support of us over the last few months, despite having hung up her competition boots a little while ago! All ready for the off, ponies on and off we go! WAIT – 'Check the trailer lights will you?!' Sure enough 15 minutes later, we were watching the course video in a garage whilst being fixed up by some odd looking chaps - our ponies stood munching hay on the back! Off we went again...

BLOODY RAINING!!! Can you believe it?! What ever next? We toyed with turning around a few times... Any excuse! No such luck, we arrived and registered and sat about chuckling, trying to banish the nerves. It worked, a little too well, as with only 25 minutes to go we decided it might be an idea to get ready and get warmed up!! IDIOTS!! What a bloody stupid thing to do – My horse needs a bit of time to get his confidence XC and I should have been ready long before getting on with only 2 riders to go before us!

Now the nerves that weren't present in the last 24 hours double barrelled me in the guts...I was (for want of a better word) B*STARDING USELESS...I relied solely on my sidekick to lead the way while Pat jinked and spooked at every bloody jump for the first 5 fences and I sat there inadequately riding EVERY fence! What a let-down I was to him – he deserved much more from me.

I'm pretty sure the long gallop down to fences 6 and 7 woke me up a bit because I suddenly felt awake again. I actually stopped passengering and started riding!!

We were flying once more, feeling confident and galloping and soaring over each obstacle – I love this horse beyond belief when we become one together going cross country – it is the most magical feeling that you simply cannot put into words. We are quite simply made for each other, both taking a little coaxing to come into our own.

Sh*t – The bloody great Trakehner♥...hold on – 3, 2, 1.. Kick kick!! I hear screams ahead... Lisa has managed to go flying into orbit at the last minute, hanging on by the seat of her unstained pants.... SIT UP, SIT UP!!! Crikey she did well to stick on...regaining her balance, we entered the woods for fence 16 (quite a meaty fallen oak trunk) – She was belly-aching about not being able to find her stirrup and was trying desperately to turn a circle ...KICK ON – Forget it... bloody Pat The Pony locked onto the log and barged Lisa and little Maggie over the jump whether they were wanting to go or not!!! I had assumed, at this point that she had regained her missing pedal and flew on to the next 3 fences and home!!

WOO BLOODY HOO!!!! Home – Fast, Alive and so desperately happy that I had regained some level of riding prowess over the course – I turned to my rather red faced, panting chum and inappropriately couldn't control my laughter!!!! Her stirrup wasn't retrievable for the last 4 fences because it had in fact flown out of the bar and was hanging miles below the saddle, dangling under the pony!!!! What a trooper!!

We walked the horses off, sponged down and had a glass of fizz before we headed off to see how we had done. Well...WOULD YOU BLOODY BELIEVE IT....We were one of the only pairs clear and inside the time!!! By 23 seconds no less! FIRST

PLACE!!!! Let the squealing commence!!!! I was elated, not just for me but for my trier of a horse, for my super-duper sidekick and for everyone that wished us luck with words of support.

We did it!!! I cannot tell you how amazing it feels to be doing this and doing it at an 'above par' standard to be getting placed! Thank you, as always, to every single one of you that has us in their thoughts and wishes us luck – It keeps me going in times of (undergarment staining) crisis – This red ribbon, hopefully one of many, belongs to you.

Louise Hosking "I've been talking about you to my friends and we can relate to you, it's great to know I'm not the only one who's not as 'ballsy' as I used to be. Keep the stories coming! X"

November 2016

November 2, 2016

ASTON PREP!

Twitchy bum time!!!!!!!!!!!!!!!!!!! The palpitations have started, the toilet trips have increased tenfold and I'm struggling to move the mouse due to the gallon of sweat pouring from my palms!!! - It can only mean one thing... THE TIMES ARE OUT!!!! My Second BE, this time at 90cms... Am I mental? I think probably YES!

November 3, 2016

LAST NIGHT... Pat was just utterly phenomenal - it was dark, freezing and usually the WASURK♥ will come out a bit tight and try and have me off at least once with a monster spook! He's started on a new supplement last week - wondering if it's already working its magic on his body? Either way, I wrote a little poem to sum up my evening, turn the page and enjoy!!

Out of the office bang on 5,

Just down the road to the yard I drive.

Walk down the field to catch him in,

The tw@t trots off, and I just grin.

Finally in, I tack him up,

And quickly down a champagne cup.

Throw on my gloves and boots and hat

And trembling, get on said tw@t!

Down in the school, a bulb flashed on,

He's soft and loose - surely a con?

Right from the off, back up, head low

I feel like Charlotte and this ere' tw@t's Valegro!!

20 minutes is all it took,

I got off and stood and shook.

The fear I feel, the nerves, the strife,

All put aside for the best ride of my life.

Diary of A Wimpy Eventer *I'm here for you every step of the way!! If I have learnt anything these last few months it's that, with Tena lady, Imodium and a good dose of alcohol - ANYTHING is possible xxx*

7th November 2016

A tale of two halves! - Our BE90 DEBUT!!

So, the morning of my much anticipated trip up to Aston Le Walls for our step up to BE 90 crept up far faster than I could have ever imagined. I'm pretty sure it left me a little flabbergasted and unprepared, but consequently less panicking time for sure! The times came out and that's when I really felt it. I was seriously scared this time. Not even about the event but about the overhaul to travel the furthest I have been to a competition, stabling my precious boy overnight somewhere new and then remembering what the bloody hell I am meant to be doing when I get there!!

We set off at 10.30am, packed and frightened. I do remember thinking far more than once; 'is it unacceptable to neck this whole bottle of port before 11am?' – Probably!! It poured with rain the WHOLE way…assume foetal position and begin rocking at the thought of running cross country in a slurry of mud from the 3 sections of riders on the course before me!! Bright bloody sunshine and not a dribble of the wet stuff on the grounds of the beautiful Aston le Walls venue!

My trusty sidekick, Lisa had been a sneaky beaky and arranged for us to have a little mini lesson with the one and only, Nigel Taylor. Unbeknown to me, this guy has done 15 Badmintons and here he was babying us round a series of frigging twigs in comparison! B*stard horse was spooking and jinking at everything, making me look like a true professional HA!…KNOB!!! Bugger it…what will be will be tomorrow!! Ponies tucked up in their overnight accommodation and us into our plush spa hotel avec Jacuzzi – we got an early night ready for a 6.30am alarm.

Alarm… Don't be bloody daft, when you are trembling enough to wake the dead at 5am, who needs an alarm!! Dressed, wretching bile and pale faced, we headed to the yard to get ready for the impending and almost certain death of the day ahead. Poor Lisa – I think it's possibly catching – mildly contagious if nothing else – she was struggling to plait through the pain of her broken finger and trembling hands – team work ensued!! All plaited and ready, we loaded up and off we went, both of us ready to turn for home.

My dressage was 9.49 am – I was trialling a new calmer today– Equine America Super So Kalm Paste?! – I should have took it myself, Pat was the calmest he had ever been in a dressage warm up in what felt like -5 degrees!! Arse, Cr*p, Bum flaps... I'm being called in… Literally needing a poo just re-living it!!

Well, what an anti-climax, It was FINE…again, nothing overly to write home about – I'm struggling to really know what the BE judges expect from the dressage phase as this is barely a Prelim and I'm getting near on 75 percent at Novice and mid-high 60's at Elementary and still only a 33 today?! Still, we live and learn.

Boots on, stirrups up and off to the show jumping warm up. Warmed up the same as Littleton, a couple of pingy jumps and off we went down to the arena. WELL what a bloody joke!!! Came up to number one, a rustic oxer with a ray of light shining on half of it, Pat wasn't looking or paying attention and spooked at the light just at the last minute, resulting in a bloody great kick from me which sent the back rail into orbit. Number 2 was a simple upright, washing lines and disorganisation meant we had that one as well. He HATES touching poles so was exceedingly upset now. Number 3 he literally breathed on the back rail this time and it fell!!! Spooked like a retard at number 4 b!!! Literally, two very small flowery fillers combined with the earlier upset meant another unwanted kick up the arse and landed another pole. Got our act together for the rest and jumped 5 through to 10 without too much hassle! WHAT A BLOODY ARSING BUMMER!!! I was very sad with 16 jumping penalties to add to our dressage score. Very sad indeed, he's a great little jumping horse and I felt he was unprepared and I didn't think about the canter, the turns, the striding NOTHING – Nerves took over and apparently the autopilot switch is far too close to the 'ride like a retard' switch. ARGH.

Back at the box, I had 20 minutes to change, smoke a few cigarettes and drain a glass of Prosecco before we had to go warm up for the death phase♥. I gulped as I saw the other riders in the warm up looking very bold and nowhere near as green in the face as me. Four to go before me and I was up… being counted down is possibly my worst nightmare, it's like being walked through the paces on the plank before you're thrown over-board. And over we went – over the first and through a gap in the hedge to number 2, he spooked – I smacked him on the shoulder to get his attention back on the job! Number 3, he spooked like a good un' again, lost my stirrup at 4 – F*cks sake - I felt all over the bloody place!! LITERALLY felt like I was going to die at any moment!! 6 was the water, got my stirrup back and started flying… 7 A and B; up and down the steps to a house as part C – BRILLIANT… Number 8; I was worried about – looked a bit big to me… he stood right off and we embraced the beloved FLIER……WOOOOOOOOOOOOOOHOOOOOOOOOOO we were FLYING!!!

9, 10, 11 a double with the second bit a skinny, no dramas, 12, 13 – a skinny log to coffin – bloody flew it – didn't even look!! GOOSEBUMPS ALL OVER ME RIGHT NOW!!! To the flying finish of an angled brush – and we were HOME and more importantly ALIVE!!!! What a bloody horse!! Utterly redeemed ourselves to end our very short BE season FLYING clear inside the time at 90cms!!!

Looking back, I am still miffed about the 4 poles that we had down, still questioning the rationality of a 33 dressage but absolutely, 100% beaming over the fact that this little horse has done a grand total of 3 cross country rounds in his life and this one my friends, was un-bloody-believable!! I've said it before and I will bang the same drum until my arms fall off – I LOVE MY ABSOLUTE LEGEND OF A HORSE now and forever more, AMEN!!!!

8th October 2016

I've only gone and won a TROPHY!!!

With the eventing season drawing to a close, I turn my attention to my secret love of dressage! Over two months ago, Pat and I had a double win at Novice and Elementary which qualified us for a Championship. Ludicrously bad timing in that it fell the day after our BE90 debut at Aston Le Walls! I put him out in the field early so the poor bugger could walk off any 'stiffys' he had from the previous day and dragged him back in at 11am for our hack to the championships! Arrived in lots of time and very slowly warmed up with lots of stretching to coax his tired muscles into some sort of organised outline!

Into the first test N34 – well, beaming the whole way round – I thoroughly enjoyed myself! I don't much like doing Novice or Elementary in a 20m x 40m sized arena anymore now, but if we just breathe and keep it collected – we make it – just about! And isn't that what it's about?! – No dry mouth, no sweating, no near death experiences, just breathing and enjoying it! We nailed it for a 73.8% just pipped to the Championship slot by 1.5% - Thrilled with my clever tired boy.

The second test was somewhat more of a challenge fitting the tough Elementary into a 20m x 40m arena is no mean feat! Pat was quite tired now and I had to use my spurs a little more than I like to :(But we got there – even the 'very nearly' wrong direction leg yield didn't put us out of kilter! For a 65% test – our neatest

Elementary to date in a short arena. We shared first place on a 65% and got a HUGE trophy for winning the Elementary league. I am so delighted and proud that he tried so hard for me after such a busy weekend. I would love to just say a MASSIVE thank you to my dear devoted husband for videoing and keeping the pony mint supplies up and once again to my absolute pleasure of a horse for just being you xxx

10th November 2016

So, is it just me or does anyone else feel SUPER deflated this week!? I'm really struggling, not with nerves but with motivation.... AND I just looked into the mirror of my Clinique compact and CHRIST ON A BIKE... I have some serious WRINKLES!!!!!!!!!!!!!!!! This weekend is going to be spent on ME. I need a haircut, facial and no stress of competing - it will be our first weekend off in ages so I think it's well deserved. I saved up a bit of money working 3 jobs last month so I think I've earned it.

She says, looking at the entries for the Arena Eventing on Saturday

GIVE IT A REST WOMAN!!

11th November 2016

Despite having a relaxing Saturday planned to include;

9.30 AM - Hair appointment

11.45 AM - Facial

1 PM - Snoozing with cats on the sofa appointment

3 PM - Sleeping after eating my body weight in mince pies.

I had 3 glasses of Malbec last night down the local and Daddy Carrot convinced me to enter the arena eventing at Coombelands on Saturday.

In the cold and (almost) sober light of day - the times have just been released and I am first to go at 9am and I am WELL AND TRULY SH*TTING MY KNICKERS!!!!!!!!!!!!!!!!!!!!!

No time to watch anyone go first, no time to cry and look presentable afterwards - I'm trembling, had 4 cigarettes and 2 poo's in the space of half an hour!!! WHAT A KNOBHEAD.

On the plus, I've managed to get my hair appointment changed to 11.30 and my facial at 1.30, let's hope I'm not carted off in an ambulance and miss them both!!!!

12th November 2016

I'm alive!!!!!!

So, last night Daddy Carrot and I went down to the sand school with Pat to make a half-hearted attempt at gearing up for today's arena eventing... put in the terrifying 'blue barrels of doom' and he was blindingly fabulous... pingy and calm and I was so enjoying myself after not riding since the dressage last Sunday.

One more time over the barrels and Bang!! 3 strides later and my darling horse is on 3 legs. My heart stopped for what felt like an eternity. My first thought was damage to a tendon.

I dived off and he's holding up his left front leg like he's hailing a f*cking taxi!!! My pride and joy, how stupid could I have been to give him 4 days off and then do some jumps.

On second and less panicky inspection he's lost a bloody shoe!!!!! Pulled it clean off, no broken bits of hoof, no nails left in the foot;

a clean swift pull of a shoe. I own an almost full thoroughbred and for those that don't or never have, losing a shoe for this particular type of horse is like having 46 strands of barbed wire pulled tight round his leg!! Drama Queen!! But what a relief!!!! Farrier booked for 7.30am tomorrow morning, we headed to the pub!!

Woke up early but not too nervous, managed to stuff a mini mince pie in my chops AND have a cup of tea! Up at the yard, mucked out and shoe back on, it started pouring with rain!! We hacked the 35 min trip to the venue and as I was FIRST to go at 9am, walked the course and got our acts together! We were soaked!!! And freezing :(but... I went in smiling as usual and jumped the first 6 show jumps CLEAR!!!!!!!!

The next 10 were mock cross country jumps and bugger me they were spooky and all over the place!! I jumped number 10, now where the bloody hell am I going?! Lost!!! Very sheepishly got my bearings and completed our first ever arena eventing CLEAR, if a little steady!

Putting to bed any demons of knocking down 4 jumps last weekend and feeling utterly elated, I was slow but who gives a fat rat's ass!!!! My horse was brilliant today, true class and truly bloody brilliant!!! 💜 💜

I don't imagine we were placed so I won't head back up in the rain.

Just thawing out before my hair appointment and girly rest of the day xx

Andi Bellini Palmadessa *"I so enjoy your posts!! You're the real deal and you keep it that way!!! Win or lose, it's how you play the game!! I think you're attitude is so refreshing in what is sometimes a very shallow world. Keep it up!!Job well done... Both of you 🐾 "*

14th November 2016

I think it's high time you knew a little more about me… I am an open book it seems!

Born Victoria Ingamells on 5th April 1986 in Boston, Lincolnshire. I grew up in a small cottage on a farming estate in Blankney, with my Mum, my Dad, 2 older brothers and an older sister.

I first sat on a pony at the age of 7 and after much begging I had fortnightly lessons at a riding school for 3 years to prove my dedication. After the addiction hit, I began helping with the hunt horses at a local private hunt yard. At 12, I started working as a cover groom for that private hunt yard, 1.5 days a week and cubbing/hunting as often as a school sick note allowed.

I learnt from some of the most knowledgeably old fashioned horse people in the industry of how to foal, feed, train and run (like clockwork) a busy yard filled with big athletes. For that opportunity, I will remain eternally grateful.

I trained and received the Pony Club tests and taught for a few years (signed off my BHSAI hours), ran various yards from polo to dressage and everything in between. I competed for a local family, a handful of event horses - Most of them are my dear shining stars in the sky now.

Around all of this I studied; blagged 14 GCSE's, 5 A levels and the most part of a BA (hons) degree in Marketing and PR. After a series of sh*t jobs, landed a good one, and I bought my very first horse at the age of 24.

The rest is history really! I am a funny creature of habit, I laugh often and rarely hide emotion. I love so much of the world and know which bits I don't. I have grown up under the watchful eyes of so many people I have come to have such huge respect for, those people shaped me into something I can be proud of. I am proud of who I am. Please make sure you are too.

Diary of A Wimpy Eventer *I'm so glad to be any kind of inspiration to anyone. We can all do this, it's in all of us to be brave. We just need the support of each other and a good wine xxxx*

21st November 2016

Mondays' Musing

I have a lot to be exceedingly grateful for. I have a super horse. I begrudge nothing about getting up an hour early to traipse out into the cold and often damp countryside before daylight. I sacrifice lovely long nails and flowing hair for a gallop across a field. Something that certainly wasn't genetic, but somehow has ingrained itself into my DNA, I live and breathe horses. Equestrian thoughts fill at least 72.4% of my daily thought process. Nearly everything I have notably achieved in life inevitably boils down to horses. They make me who I am.

People that don't think about horses or that don't have horses in their lives, will struggle to understand just HOW important scouring eBay for 'equestrian items ending soonest' truly is to us.

My long-suffering non-horsey husband understands. He understands that I am stark-raving bonkers and that if he visits the horse once a week he will get home-made baked goods and a hassle free existence!

I guess what I am trying to say is; that despite how sh*t it feels waking up on a Monday and dragging my unenthusiastic arse into the office, I have a lot to look forward to. Next year we are embarking on greatness, on a crusade to eventing success and non-death... I MUST try harder to spend this winter preparing as best I can and that starts with attitude.

Join me EVERYONE - Shake off the Monday blues, be positive, sit up straighter, breathe in deeper and stick a middle finger up to anyone that tiddles on your toast (your boss excluded). Have a bloody cake if you want one, smoke a cigarette if you want to - be content and feel great - because we are, in our own individual way, bloody super at something!

I feel better already.

Have a super day!

xxx

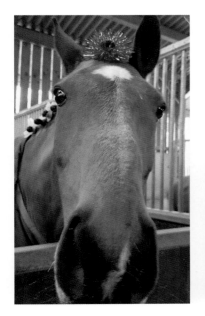

Photo by LRG Photography

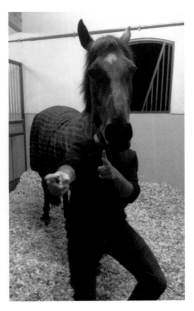

Photo by LRG Photography

December 2016

11th December 2016

So a little weekend round up from us....

SATURDAY

I have been SO careful with Pat after his scary shoe pulling injury that left me counting every single lucky star in the sky. Saturday we planned a hack with our new yard buddies Auntie Nugget and her horse, Div (Auntie Nugget – because she always has a pocket full of pony treat nuggets at the ready!). 2.30pm, swig of port and off we went. An hour passed full of chatter and giggling... this is vital to our confidence development, having people to enjoy the journey with but wait... we were LOST!!! B*llocks! Got a mild wrist slap from a local land owner for trespassing and we back tracked home!! I did manage to fly a hunt jump en route though and Pat felt mega!!!

Home just as dusk set in, cuddles for Pat, dinner and back into the warm.

SUNDAY

Today was exceptionally vomit inducing for me. I had planned to jump today, the first time since the shoe pulling... I felt sick to my stomach building a double and parallel, I smoked a nervous cigarette and went down to the arena.

I did 3 cross poles before I stopped swallowing bile. Popped them up a bit and got my act together. Jumped very nicely through a 95/1m combination and I wasn't sick... result!!! He feels bloody fabulous, soft and confident and I just love him so so much

I also have a very odd stigma with taking off anything that appears to have brought me luck... now this might sound borderline psychotic but over 2 months ago, I put on a Mojo wristband...

now, I'm not overly fashionable but I do feel a little bit like one of those people that go to festivals when I'm wearing it!!! My 17 year old niece might possibly think it's cool! Now, I am usually the clumsiest, bruise covered liability, I think the ratio of bruise to normal skin on my shins has improved since and I haven't died whilst wearing it so, those 2 things has qualified it as a constant fixture on my arm.

I'm feeling happy, planning to go somewhere at the weekend show wise so I'll keep you posted when I've found one

Night guys

xxx

14th December 2016

I want every single one of us to feel immensely proud of what we have achieved. Just little things, day to day that make us feel proud and great. I want everyone to post at least 1 picture (below in the comments if you like or share it with friends) of how far we have come in our form of dressage/schooling/staying on whilst attempting to do sitting trot.

After all, we are all in this together, we all smell a little bit like wee, have been trodden on and cried with frustration over our passion for horses. We are all individually achieving something every day... blow your own bloody trumpet for a change without feeling like you're being judged for it!!!

This post unbelievably received over 250 images of people being proud of themselves – I couldn't be happier! *

18th December 2016

I woke up this morning with the biggest bout of crippling nerves I have had for months. I've not felt like this for ages, I think having a few weeks off from shows has made me feel somewhat inadequate as a rider and out in public; 100% worse!!!! – I was only going to a bloody dressage show!

I arrived at the yard and got ready, plaited, tinselled and dressed up like a prize winning turkey. We trundled off to Brinsbury for the Riding Club winter dressage series. Now, after a rare lesson yesterday I couldn't face the Medium 71 class that I had originally entered. We just aren't good enough yet. Simple.

I have taught my own horse from scratch, I don't know how to be better than we are right now, so I need help. My knowledge and skills stop at very basic lateral (sideways fancy) movements. I just didn't feel right pushing my poor horse all over the place and feeling like we didn't achieve something so I entered the novice non-competitively and remained in the Elementary. And as it was a festive occassion and as I am not one to blend into the background, I dressed up in full Santa costume and Pat dressed as Rudolph!

Now I had dulled the nerves with a 9am port swig, I felt festive and ready to rock!! Thanks to my super smashing yard owners, we got a surprise Christmas lift in their lovely horsebox ... I always feel like royalty sitting on the crisscross leather seats and struggling with no transport for what has felt like forever, this was a lovely treat! Plenty of time to settle in now I wasn't hacking there so we had a jump round the clear round course for a lovely clear and pretty rosette (that's now on the Christmas tree). Woohoo!!

Into the Novice test, I felt smiley and as if by magic... Pat went super!!! We broke into canter in the medium trot but f*ck it... can't be perfect all the time can we?! As I wasn't riding competitively in the Novice class there was no placing. I finished on a shade under 74 percent which is consistent for him at this level. I was immensely thrilled with a 9 for my free walk again, something I have massively focussed on because of its double marks!! Very happy with that indeed.

I didn't bother going back down to the warm up before the Elementary test, there were only 3 in it so not long to wait!

Apart from one small blip and rider satnav error, it wasn't a shambles. He should have been more connected and off my leg but I wasn't displeased. I untacked and popped up for my sheet, thoroughly convinced of 3rd place (The other 2 competitors were very strong). I literally couldn't contain myself when the rosette I was handed was RED!!!! I even double checked the name on the sheet it was pinned to!!

Tears rolling down my face, I just couldn't believe it. My beautiful darling horse after scaring me senseless with that leg only 4 weeks ago, has come out and been utterly amazing yet again. I cannot put into words how lucky I feel to see my best friend, my lovely team mate in this sport of equestrianism, doing such a phenomenal job of bobbling me around and collecting all these red rosettes. Crying again now!!!!

Thanks to every single one of you for your endless support, to Auntie Nugget for calling our tests so well, to Mark and Alison for your help, support and flashy taxi and to my lovely darling husband for towing the line when I smell so bad and put out so infrequently!

We've only bloody gone and done it again!!!!!

Maz Turvey *Amazing nothing more to be said xx*

23rd December 2016

Pat and I would like to wish you all a very happy Christmas Eve
Eve in the form of a very poorly performed take on the traditional
favourite – Once in Royal David's City!!!! Xxxx

The lyrics if you want to sing along....

Once there was an Irish pony

Backed in Ireland and sold on

He was young and weak and lonely

Until his new friend came along

He was small and very kind

Taught this girl that love is blind.

We rode over jumps and ditches

Went to shows collecting wins

Then one day the girl was frightened

By the pony's lively pings!

Though she loved him without fail

She toyed with placing him for sale

BUT…Booze and blogging made her braver

And decided to plough on

Got back on her wondrous pony

No looking back, their love still strong.

So here we are, the eve of bravery

Attempting to event all year

Wish us luck and health and safety

As we conquer our last fear.

That love I feel for this dear pony

May it guide us home once more.

xxx

Alison Payne *You are officially the maddest person I know!! Will play this to Pat tomorrow morning xx*

27th December 2016

Today, I feel exceptionally lucky to have found such a wonderful yard with kind and non-judgemental people on it. I just want to stress how important that is to all of us. For the last 7 years at least, I have learnt to grow an extremely thick skin and plead ignorance despite my wealth of equestrian knowledge and experience. I do this to secure my failings and not make anyone feel inferior. No one likes a 'know it all', least of all me!

I don't give two sh*ts these days if anyone thinks I'm completely clueless, that I can't ride well or my horse isn't reaching his potential- b*llocks to them!

Read it carefully - Those that mind don't matter and those that matter don't mind. Please keep that in mind when people p*ss on your chips!

Bloody well enjoy your horses, fall off, get scared (terrified) and overcome your fears step by step. We can all be super - just one day at a time.

Caroline Boyd *"So true. We need to tell ourselves this more often."*

Lois Springer *"Words to live by!"*

31st December 2016

A post of reflection...

At the start of 2016 I was a trembling mess. I didn't compete and I rarely rode, NEVER hacked out and feared getting my saddle out of the tack room. I enquired about sales livery for Pat because I felt sick to my stomach at the thought of getting on him.

In July, I got married to my super supportive non-horsey husband and we moved into our new house and Pat into his.

Moving livery yards transformed us, I gained enough confidence to ride every day (Sedalin fuelled to begin with until I could feel safe again). This is where our year began - with only 4 months left!!! I went on the hunt ride as a first outing and scared myself sh*tless jumping far more than planned but it beban to fix us to an extent... every time I rode for about 6 weeks I reminded myself; if I can do that then I can do anything!

I entered a hunter trial and two days before went cross country schooling for the first time in years - I was definitely scared but more determined than ever. We successfully completed our hunter trial without death or injury.

Pat and I became best friends again, we fell in love with galloping again and he felt like he was looking after me, we were and still are, made for each other. So we entered our first BE80 at Littleton... we nailed it for 5th place and I literally couldn't have been happier. I did lots of clinics, hacking and entered the BE90 at Aston Le Walls. Despite utter terrification we did it, pooped up our SJ but mega clear and quick cross country which made me prouder than ever of how far we had come in just a few months.

We then reverted to dressage diva and won the Elementary championships, and a few more wins at Novice and Elementary level in the few weeks that followed. To yesterday, where Pat and I went to a showing show (our first one in years) and WON the riding horse class. He was impeccably behaved and made me so super proud to own this heart throb of a horse. I was riding around the ring beaming with pride and it was the first comment we received along with our rosette. How very few people ever actually look as though they are enjoying it? – I hear this all the time, just try it next time you are out; let go of the stigma, let go of the fear and enjoy it.

Today I feel lucky, proud and extremely excited to take on 2017. I absolutely couldn't do any of it without the support of my friends, family and my dearest husband. Next year is going to be an absolute blast and I cannot wait to share it with you all.

Here's to a new year, a fresh start and a dream to pursue. If you do one thing today; decide on a dream and chase it like your pants are on fire... I'm with you every step of the way.

Love as always

Vic and Pat

Xxxxx

Sarah Lee *You don't do things by halves. From not riding to competing within a few months. Inspiring, this brought tears to my eyes :)*

Annalisa Alexander *Truly inspirational! Thank you so much for sharing your journey, you've given me hope that I can overcome my nervousness after years of not riding! Bring on 2017. And I can't wait to see what you and Pat get up to!*

Linda Jones *Thank you. I love your posts as they are so positive and inspiring that 'normal' riders can achieve a dream despite a 'normal' life*

Pamela Rutterford *Inspiration at its best! All the best for 2017 xx*

Maz Turvey *Wow, an inspirational read as ever. Just shows what a little grit, determination and support can do. I had a tear in my eye reading this I must admit. 2017 I'm going to take a leaf out of your book, looking at lots of clinics and low key competition to get some confidence up and to build on the relationship Ebony and I have. Looking forward to seeing what you guys get up to next year. Happy New Year xxx*

January 2017

4th January 2017

Today I am suffering the effects of last night's 25 minutes without stirrups. My thighs hurt, my tummy hurts, my minky♥ hurts (damn gel seat saver rubadubbed my girly bits!). Now I know it was 'No Stirrup November' but we were off games then, so I am bringing you - JOYFULLY JIGGLING JANUARY.

Jiggle away my fellow followers, jiggle until you joggle! I am determined to get good at this!

.....Oh and did I mention... I've just put my name down for DRAG HUNTING on SUNDAY 😱 😱 😱 😱 😱 😱 😱 😱 Holy mother of crumbles... what have I done - I've had to take 2 poo breaks just filling out the disclaimer!!!

Gemma Conroy *I can only suggest sudocreme.... before and after!*

7th January 2017

Just a small musing from the bottom of my tea cup this morning, how I wish I could sleep in, but every part of my human wants to get up and start the day in the hour of 5!!!

I was just checking in on Instagram and stumbled across an account which shall go unnamed! I browsed picture after picture of what appeared to be success, beauty and style. I spent 20 minutes mentally deciding that now it's 2017, maybe I should consider being more stylish, more on trend, thinner and with nicer hair?! The crux of it is - I go through this thought process about 3 times a week!!! I wish I could be more like someone else for a brief flashing moment.

Now, if there someone browsing my social media accounts wishing they were a fuzzy, ginger, marginally overweight nutbar with a seemingly average existence?! Ha, like hell!

I think what we all must celebrate in ourselves is our individual pretties. There has to be much less shame in loving something about yourself - without someone slapping an 'Arrogant Tw*t' sticker on your forehead!! We are all individuals, bloody fabulous for something... crikey, it might only be something small but I bet you know what it is deep down.

I personally happen to think that I have a sparkling sense of humour, alright I'm not a stick thin, large bosomed goddess in designer clothes nor am I a wealthy or an overly intelligent business woman... but I am me and instead of spending this year wishing I was more like someone else, I am going to love being more like me every day.

Please love who you are and don't you dare feel ashamed of it!!!! Go on... celebrate and share your inner pretties, bugger what anyone else thinks!!!

Have a brilliant day... I'm going to hack or jump, can't decide, and then get ready for dying on the hunting field tomorrow!!

Xxxx

8th January 2017

So, let's go back to this morning...

I got up and drove to the yard un-phased at this point, to skip out, give Pat some hay and not think about the day ahead. Back at home I actually ate breakfast... grilled mushrooms, tomato, avocado and a poached egg (still on the post-Christmas diet).

The Kent and Surrey Bloodhounds were meeting locally to the yard at 12.30pm (with a half hour hack and chain smoke to factor in) I needed to be plaited and ready for death by 11.45am! Bang on 10 my belly was jiggly, swallowed two Imodium and sat on the toilet for a while and I was right as rain! Constipation for a few days is a small fee to pay in comparison to soiling yourself in front of 50 people you don't know!! Plus getting faeces out of my new gel seat saver would have been royally tedious!!

Off we went, swigging at the hip flask and puffing on a (almost quit) cigarette, trundled down to the meet. It was already fairly busy and Pat seemed a bit of a frisky biscuit when I tried to accept my compulsory port snifter! Downed it and minutes later we were off!

GALLOPING was Pats pace of choice for the day, he was mega strong and likes to be up at the front, so that's where we stayed until he settled. We had a line of cantering and trotting with a blast down the gallops to warm us up before I heard the smasher of a Field Master♥ say that the next line might get a bit exciting!

I was cr*pping myself at that point if I'm brutally honest!!

Covered in mud already, hip flask pretty much empty, lines 2&3 did not disappoint on the excitement stakes! We jumped 4ft hedge after 4ft hedge one after the other... big bloody bushy great hedges!!! And I tell you what, I was absolutely blinking loving it!!!! Christ on a bike, my tiny boy grew wings... we were flying! I cannot tell you what it felt like!!! I was crying with joy and pride soaring round those fields, until we turned and landed ourselves in front of a metal five bar gate, imagine my horror!!

Bum twitching, I kicked for a good stride and we sailed it, so big in fact, that I almost come off the back! Bugger me this was better than anything I have ever done in my entire life... we finished the 4th and last line with a huge 5ft box hedge with a 7ft drop on landing and came home with the biggest grin on the entire hunting field!!!

I cannot tell you all how today has made me feel, I seriously love the absolute bones of that tiny Trojan flying machine, he made me so blinking proud today. Looked after me good and proper.

I must also say that I have hunted a lot in my youth but absolute hats off to the Kent and Surrey Bloodhounds you have given me the best day of my life today and here I sit in my bubbly bath with a husband made cup of tea, not quite believing what we have done this afternoon.

Can you honestly believe that this time last year I couldn't even get on my horse through fear, and now bloody look at us!!!!!! Here's to a very, very wonderful horse and an exciting year ahead!!

Love, best wishes and thank you for the endless support. I await photographic evidence from the sterling Julian Portch Photography to prove my balls were almost always intact today!

Goodnight xxxx

Grace Reed *Such an inspiration and the progress is unreal! Xx*

Lorraine Snelgrove *Sounds like you had an amazing day. Well done Vic and Pat xxx*

11th January 2017

Well, its day three of post-hunting agony. I have been crippled for two days now. Stairs are a no-no, lowering my plump arse onto the loo seat - also dicey. Kneeling, crouching or lifting my arms above my head - forget it!

I got my leg over last night though! Good old Pat stood like a rock while I jiffled myself out of an involuntary cramp... good boy Patsy! I am still on a high though, I CAN DO THIS - Look at me - I can do it after all.

The nerves cripple me: my racing heart makes me dizzy, the sweating makes it hard to grip the reins and the constant toilet visits make it near on impossible to get on sometimes, but these are the things I have no control over - I can control how I fight through all of it to feel that feeling I get when I'm home and alive and full of exhilaration.

16th January 2017

Monday Morning Musing.

Apparently, today is the most depressing day of the year - Blue Monday. Something about the weather, daylight hours, debt management, Christmas expenditure and New Year's resolution guilt....

I have to say, after the consumption of too much Rioja at our friends last night, I have felt better. My excessive consumption also resulted in me sucking a rubber fish to my forehead, meaning that I am now the proud owner of the biggest love bite in the middle of my face the world has ever seen. I've tried to cover it up... thanks Clinique, but it is still glowing through like the bloody 5th of November!!! When I am not having to see any more humans' bar my husband - I will be sure to post pictures for you!

Back to Blue Monday...

It all boils down to envy, we all look at other people's lives and the grass appears thick and lush and oh so green... but is it? A little insight into my life; I have 3 jobs, I leave the house at 6.30AM and come home at 7PM. I have to do the washing, cleaning, cooking, food shopping and shower before sitting down to eat (usually around 8pm). We rent an average 2 bed semi in an okay(ish) suburban area, I buy pretty much everything for Pat second hand, I don't have a nice car or savings and we don't go on holiday much or have expensive clothes. I have no transport for Pat so I work those extra jobs to be able to fund the whacking costs of dream chasing. I am tired, always crashing out straight after tea. BUT would I change it? Would I want to have everything handed to me on a plate or have none of it at all and live in a burrow in the woods?

What I am trying to say is, think of everything you do to get to where you are, the sacrifices you make for your horses, hobbies, children that make us so tremendously happy and, at times, tremendously sad. Be proud of where you are right now at this time of life, look to the future with hope, not dread. Be bold in your decisions to better that hopeful life - and try to worry less when plans take a turn off piste - My husband said, just yesterday; "The plan can change 100 times, it's the goal that must remain the same."

Be brave, enjoy it and love the life you have - don't wish you were someone else, one day you might be and you might not be happier at all.

B*llocks to you Blue Monday... I'm off to dance in the drizzle with a fag!!

Have a lovely day xxx

17th January 2017

Bloody stinker of a day that has been absolutely saved by the humanity and kindness of ... wait for it... an eBay seller.

As I mentioned, I'm not rolling in money and I have been saving up, starting this month for a little toot toot for Pat and I to go on our adventures in. Now I wasn't looking for a bloody Oakley Supreme, just a little 3.5t runner to suit my moth infested wallet.

Well I found the perfect one only 2 months too soon!!! It's a dear little box only half an hour away but as I don't have the money, I thought a heartfelt message might not hurt. The minute I pressed send I regretted it, thinking that I would get my heart crushed by a 'tyre kicker' boulder being thrown at me. Instead what I got was the loveliest reply, asking how much I could afford and how long I would need to get the rest!! Now, I'm not sure I have lost my faith in human kind over the years or whether you just get more cynical with age but, I am truly touched.

The reality is, this kind lovely lady doesn't deserve not to be paid in full so I'm wracking my brains on how to find the money. I am not terribly sexy, so selling my body is sure to end in failure and I have nothing but my overweight cat that I could sell to a blind man wanting a walrus (he might be hard to find), in order to fund my toot.

If anyone has any other bright ideas... please feel free to share them, I'm open to wandering down all avenues... oh and I can perform at weddings, funerals, christenings... I'm great at fitting 12 Pringles in my mouth at once and it makes for a great filler between speeches/first dance!

Love as always

Vic

Ps - Pat enjoyed his first day in the big boy fields and was very happy about this.

Xxxx

20th January 2017

You know sometimes, when things just get to you?!

Quite often I feel it, when the morning alarm goes off on my husband's side of the bed and due to earplugs, it takes him an AGE to turn it off - in the mean time I am laying there imagining the quickest, and easiest way I could wrap the cord of the alarm clock around his neck without having to move from under the covers...

Or, when your boss has categorically told you he is going to be out of the office and you pull into the car park and see his car parked there. Never more have I wanted to ram my tiny sh*tmobile into the back of his car, faking an injury worthy of a sick note!

Yesterday was one of those days for me. After the elation of finding a potential source of funding for my budget Pony Wheels, booking a viewing for tomorrow morning and trying desperately not to let out a bit of wee... I received a message telling me that THEY F*CKING SOLD IT!! I totally understand, I do. The lovely lady explained that she needed the money and couldn't wait - but BOY was I blue about it!

I also got to the yard to find that my bird brain of a horse had over-reached AGAIN... When will I learn to keep the bloody boots on AT ALL TIMES!! Sliced into the bulb of his heel and is now the proud owner of a sick note and blue bandaged foot... Could it have got any worse?!

Well no - it didn't, I got home, my husband had bought flowers without knowing about any of the days sh*t storm of events, I broke my mid-week drinking resolution - RESULT, and none of the cats had left a hair ball on the floor...

The moral of the story is - if things don't go your way, it wasn't your way to go.

Read that last line again. Don't feel sad or disappointed, just find another way to go...

Enjoy today, it's Friday after all, go make a cuppa, have a biscuit, do a star jump with one hand on your bosom (in secret... you'll laugh - trust me) - I want updates of your weekend plans - mine are writing and looking for things to sell!!! Pat's got his sick note in hand so might get a brush if he's lucky!!

Love, as always

Vic and Pat

xxx

January 24, 2017

I'd like to talk a little seriously for a minute - Not like me, I know - but I just read something and it got me thinking...

About something that we will all have experienced in some form or another...

Certain words, like rape or cancer, make us wince inside right to our very core. This topic does the same for many people I am sure

BULLYING

The question on everyone's lips is 'How dare people think they can get away with making others feel so terrible?'

Now, it comes in many forms and I won't openly share too much detail, but I have been on the end of the bullying stick and being a sensitive soul, not always been able to handle it. The crux of it is, and it took me a long time to see the light, the only thing you can really do is rise above it. There are several ways to do this but realisation of ONE very simple thing is KEY - You will NEVER stop rivalry, jealousy or bitterness that is caused by the resentment of other people's success.

SUCCESS - that word right there. You are being targeted because someone feels INFERIOR to you. Think about that - really think about it, the person being a chip p*sser is actually aware that you have something they don't. Feel proud of that and lift your bloody head up. Don't fret on it when you get home - don't!

You see, bringing people down only makes a 'bully' feel better for a short time - then they are filled with self-loathing or left unfulfilled completely - After all, they are only being mean because of their own low opinion of themselves, which is the saddest part of all. The only person that a bully is bullying, is themselves. Remember that.

I've said it before and I'll say it again - surround yourself with people that either couldn't give a sh*t, ones that would give their last sh*t to see you succeed, or the ones that don't know what sh*t you're doing and forget what the pissers say along the way - they'll wish they were nicer when you're rich and famous!!! <3 xxxxx

27th January 2017

So, it's Friday...

What a week, my head is spinning. On the Pat front - it's been stupidly cold and the school hasn't had a chance to defrost, so one pointless lunge this week is all we have managed. It's been over a week since my last ride and I'm beginning to feel violently sick thinking about getting back on - time off is my ultimate nemesis, good job the port supplies were replenished this Christmas! We had a visit from the lovely horse dentist, nothing to report just the usual file and buff!

I come to my Friday musing - Well there are 2 actually.

The first one is HARD WORK. Now, I have never really stuck at much in my life - probably not the best example but, being a typical Aries - I too much enjoy the thrill and challenge of change and new beginnings. That isn't to say I haven't worked hard because by gum... I didn't get this far without it!! It's time for a re-think - I have plans, major life changing plans this year that I am working hard to make sure I fulfil.

This year my philosophy of life is changing, I am focusing on working hard at the things I enjoy over things I don't just to make ends meet. I think that if you enjoy something, work as hard as you can possibly work at it, and you will be recognised for that and hopefully rewarded. Hey, I'd rather be poor than miserable any day, beans on toast are under-rated!

I guess what I am trying to say is - work hard for the things that matter, don't lose focus, and be the best that you can be at those things regardless of changes around you. Don't make excuses for not working as hard as you could, because only you will suffer in the end - the rewards will come in the form of success. Hard work will always give you something back - even if it's only self-gratification when you down your Friday night wine!

Now, moving onto the second musing (I just couldn't choose between them!) INSPIRATION. Hard work is all very well but sometimes when we cannot see the bloody wood for the trees, we need re-aligning. We need someone or something to make us realise why we are doing this, someone that is on the journey of dream fulfilment - it gives us hope and light at the end of the tunnel.

This week I have to highlight an extraordinary woman that I met over a few drinks, she has put her heart and soul (and available finances) into something that isn't half as rewarding as it should be right now. She isn't far from taking a turn down the dark road of defeat and needs a light shining on her path again. I want to be that light for her, for all of you, for anyone working commendably hard and not getting what they deserve.

I feel as though I have a different purpose now, to be a torch for people when they're down a dark path - I will WORK HARD at that, harder than I have worked for anything. And YOU are my INSPIRATION, all of you reading this, so thank you.

What does the weekend hold? I plan on downing my body weight in port before hacking tomorrow. Hey, if it's not frozen I might hack and do the clear round at Brinsbury College and then probably a lazy Sunday walk to the pub for a roast! Need to get my arse in gear on the little lorry fund and my BE season which kicks me in the guts in 6 weeks time!!!

Love, as always xxx

29th January 2017

Well what a bloody joke... the nerves were back with a vengeance today, I jumped 5ft hedges and galloped for my life only 3 weeks ago and the thought of hacking to a local jumping clinic has me reaching for the Imodium!! I was so so scared today, crikey I nearly had a cry getting on yesterday too but, determined to make it big this year I need to focus, focus, focus on why I'm doing this.

I hacked, uneventfully, to Brinsbury College for my 12pm slot, shared with one other poor soul. Explained to Teachy what my issues are and why I was trembling and we pop some poles and a cross to begin. Well... Pat clearly hasn't forgotten that hunting means you jump at 100 miles an hour right?! Errrrr... VERY NOT FUNNY!!! I was clinging on like a monkey and felt utterly sh*t for what felt like an eternity!

It took almost 35 minutes for him to settle, he was cornering at the rate of a superbike and it left me stirrup-less on more than one occasion. You know, I'm not sh*t, I know I'm not I just felt it today... a mega, mega massive sack of dog cr*p swinging from a stick! I think I need a re-focus from someone that knows me and Pat. He's far from a schoolmaster♥, I've taught this pony everything he knows and we've cut plenty of corners I can tell you!

We finished jumping a course which felt far worse than it looked on the video. I'm ever the critic of my own poor performance! Go take a look at the videos, feel free to tell me how cr*p I am and how I sock his back teeth out all the time, it's the reality and things I'm working on - Operation: be less sh*t commenced today!!!

So... we are back in the game again, temporarily rusty, but back! I laughed with Pat ALL the way home, out loud like a crazy person and isn't that what it's about? I love him more than life itself, he makes it all worth the regular loose leavings I can tell you.

Peace out chirps!! And thanks again for keeping me sane, keeping me going and keeping my pants unstained!!

Love as always

Vic and Pat Xxxx

30 January 2017

It's a sad day when you have to replace something you adore...

I'm in the market for a show jacket, I'm poor so not too dear. I have long arms (like a monkey) and no boobs!! I'm a 34" in other ones. I'll be wearing it 3/4 times a month so preferably something that would wash? If that exists!! And I'm going to go tweed this time not navy, I'm up for trend setting with funky bold tweed too.

So, in conclusion I need a free jacket with built in breast enlargements that self-cleans and stands out from the crowd so my husband can spot me....

Answers on a postcard please!

February 2017

2nd February 2017

Onto our first cross country training of the year…

Well…. everyone, you will be pleased to know I am alive, my pants aren't stained and I *think* we got our mojo back!!!

I feel bloody frigging fantastic!!!

Let's roll back to 8.30am… I got to the yard and mucked out, I had to have everything ready to leave for 10.30ish. Had WAY too much time on my hands and my stomach was well and truly empty from four loose deposits before breakfast, so I had a cig and started on the hip flask. Now I'd like to add, that a good chum bought me a rather nice reserve port around Christmas time and it would surely be a crying shame not to fill the flask with it for today's special outing?! It was all too easy to drink and by 10.30am I had slurped up half of my flask, not loaded the trailer and the horse wasn't ready… but crikey, I felt mega up for it!! (Cross country that is ☺). My dearest Auntie Nugget was driver today and had to put up with my nervous ramblings and poor directions for our 40 minute trip to the course!!

Pony unloaded, legged up by Daddy Carrot and we were off! Bobbling round warming up, not dying… this was ok, I think I was enjoying myself even at the start!!! A novelty!! First couple of jumps out of the way and I was bloody loving it!! Pat can be so mega spooky at times but today, I felt like I did galloping over the finish line at Aston last November, full of pride and confidence!

One thing I will say, I haven't had many lessons of late and I get scared at not feeling good enough, hats off to my newly dubbed 'Lord Fs A lot' he was the most incredible trainer, not for everyone I doubt but for me - simply perfect. Now, not many people could liken you to a dead pigeon in your approach to a fence but still fill you with confidence. He made clear that he despised my high hands and grinning all the 'b*stard time' but this guy really has skills as a superb trainer and Pat and I were on fire because of it.

We jumped a load of different stuff, never once feeling out of our depth, even over some pretty meaty monster fences!! Steps, water, ditches, we really covered everything I needed to grow my confidence today.

I came away beaming, my horse, my bloody amazing tiddler pony has done it again, I could cry with joy and relief that I didn't come out this year a snotty, tearful wreck.

Thank you Lord, Auntie Nugget, Daddy Carrot and most importantly, thank you Pat - you are simply the best thing I could ever, ever wish for 💜 💜 xxxx

Over and out 😳 xx

PS - the Champion Equestrian Wear body protector I am trialling was 100% by far the best I have ever owned, my tiny boobies weren't crushed by the armour and doing up the zip didn't force vomit into my throat – Result! I will treasure it for all eternity 😊

3rd February 2017

I'm still high as a kite from yesterday, this is exactly why we do it right?! If anyone is in any doubt of whether they should stretch out over their comfortable boundaries, you should, because the euphoria lasts for days!!!

Like I always say, it's better than sex on a bed of money with a Lindt chocolate in my mouth!!! 😆

7th February 2017

TUESDAY - A lot of people's worst day of the week - you've painfully dragged your arse through the sheer agony of Monday and then Tuesday's bristly palm smacks you right across the chops!

Today, Tuesday started just like that for me - I broke the Non-Midweek Drinking clause last night because of the worst Monday of 2017 to date, so I felt less than up for 8 hours of office boredom when my husband finally stopped hitting that bloody snooze button!!

I felt downright unmotivated, something needed to change, like I need a darn good shake up in life, so after some excellent advice - I have set to work on a plan. If you too, are feeling like life is going nowhere and that you are stuck in a big fat rut, ask yourself...

What are the causes of your unhappiness/unfulfillment?

For me, it is full time office work - I feel trapped in the limbo of PAYE and Self-Employment. I am frustrated to the point of despair! For once, the horse side of life is playing second fiddle to this - I cannot be happy, confident and achieve my horsey dreams if this part of my life is a crumbly bumbly biscuit!

What would make you happiest, what is the main thing you would like to achieve?

This is simple for me - I LOVE to write, I love it. I laugh as I write, I cry when I read my writing back to myself, the emotion it brings out in me, the sheer joy I get from inspiring others. I cannot tell you how happy I am writing to an audience that appreciates my terrible knee jerk sense of humour and heart on sleeve honesty.

I'd also like to be dictating my hours a bit more, have more time with Pat and enjoy him more.

By outlining goals, breaking them down into achievable milestones and time-lining them, I hope I can make things happen! If you feel down, find out the cause and make a plan... baby steps remember, and soon we will all be wondering what the problem was!

I'm bursting with excitement for the future - you can be ANYTHING you want to be and you only EVER get one go at life - make it count - make a difference, and most importantly, make it happy.

Love Always

Vic xxx

10th Feb, 2017

It's Friday, My favourite time of week for a blissful musing...

Today I'd like to talk about BELIEF. Not in the religious sense, but in the 'believing in yourself' sense. Now, I am becoming an advocate of self-belief, to the point where almost every day, I have to restrain myself from physically knuckle dusting someone that doesn't have enough of it! It is VITAL and I'll tell you why...

In every aspect of our lives, in our family dynamics, in relationships, with our horses, our competitions, our work life, even fighting for the last cucumber in Tesco's, we all need some degree of self-belief. I don't think there is anything wrong with having a high opinion of yourself as long as you are gracious and polite to boot. You can only truly put others before yourself without an ulterior motive, if you have enough belief in yourself to donate a slice of it to another.

I had little to none of it 3 years ago - my confidence and self-belief, in all areas of my life, were see-through... My marriage of 6 years was over, my fleeting relationship following that marriage was a royal, great big sack of rat sh*t, my redundancy money had run out and I was forced to take a job paying less than my first ever admin role straight out of school, so I lodged with mates in order to get by. I had NOTHING going for me, Pat was the only thing I had, I couldn't afford him but I would have slept in his stable rather than give him up. I was not very happy and felt like there was nowhere to turn. It was Pat and my non-judgmental friends that helped me restore that once full pot of belief.

Now I have it back, I can see how important it is. If you believe you can - then you really, truly can. It sounds cr*p but it is true. Believing in myself meant that I could get back on Pat again, that we could enter a show again, that we could affiliate, that we could do cross country without dying, that I could meet a man that wasn't an arsehole.... I believed in myself and all of these good things, amazing wonderful things have happened.

Now, I might have been due some luck, but I know that if I didn't believe in my own abilities I would NEVER be as happy and fulfilled as I am right now. I'm genuinely fond of myself these days - I want everyone else to feel how life changing that is...

Go look in the mirror, DO IT NOW... look into your own eyeballs and find something that you like about yourself and bloody well say it out loud - be proud of who you are, don't always try to be different, you are already brilliant enough.

My weekend is going to be spent drinking from the flask of courage again as I have Arena Eventing at 11.52am tomorrow and I've just had to go for another poo just thinking about it! Have a great one (weekend, not poo) - I'll keep you posted on my hopeful non-death!

Love always

Vic and Pat xxx

14ᵗʰ February 2017

Happy Valentine's Day

Are you sick of hearing it yet....? I do think love should be celebrated, but not just for one day of the year. Let's talk about that feeling we call LOVE.

Now isn't it funny, when you fall in 'LOVE' you feel excited, fluttery in the belly and unable to stop smiling? Yet years in, it is likely you don't feel that, it leaves you a little fooled and disappointed. It doesn't mean you care any less, or feel anything less for your loved one - often you feel more, but what a shame that LOVE tricks us into thinking this is what it should feel like all the time.

I believe that you can LOVE almost anything or anyone if you let yourself. I love my husband, I love my cats, I love Pat within an inch of his tiny ears, I love my family and my friends, I love my little car, I love this blog and all of you that get something out of it. I Love Love.

HOWEVER, I am CR*P at LOVE - I mean CR*P, CR*P. I love too much, I wear my fragile heart on my cardigan sleeve and it often gets bruised or damaged by very small things people do or say. Love can hurt just as much as it can make you burst with happiness but that's what keeps us knowing we are alive and human right?!

Today, whether you are feeling IN love or despise the very bones of love, feeling anything at all means you have a heart. You care about yourself and that feeling called LOVE, celebrate THAT if nothing else today.

I LOVE YOU ALL so very much, for feeding my absolute love of helping people achieve greatness, have a wonderful day won't you? Remember to go and look in the mirror and choose something you LOVE about yourself today <3 xxx

15th February 2017

Today (slight sense of humour failure) I want to bare my soul a little in the hope that someone can offer some perspective and help me see the light...

So, as you all know, I use this page to address MASSIVE confidence issues that lurk under my pinky exterior. I uncontrollably and subconsciously tell myself, almost every day, that I am not good enough at one or more areas in my life. I am rarely ever a good enough wife, never a good enough friend, I'm a careless daughter, sibling and auntie to my beautiful nephews and nieces. I rarely give 100% at work and always know I could have done better and this all seeps through to Pat.

I get to the yard to ride and whilst I know I can get a tune out of pretty much any horse, I have a huge battle feeling like I'm just not good enough on my own. Line up 12 horses, unbroken, feral, and wild and I'd confidently give them all a go - madness huh! But give me my darling Patsy and I just melt into a soggy, terrified mess.

More often than not, I feel as though I don't really know what I'm doing - maybe it's because we have progressed to a level I have no skills in yet (it hasn't stopped us before) or maybe it is the crippling fear of him shying or having the sillies and me falling off and never waking up. Either way, I have felt this way with my own horses since, well, forever.

I'm mumbling a bit, but basically - this huge lack of confidence in the areas I care most about is gradually destroying them. My marriage, my horse, my work - I simply don't know how to feel like I am brilliant, I want to - I want to feel worthy and I want to stop feeling like I'm letting people down all the time. I'm sick to the back teeth of hearing - it's got to come from inside you... I've tried - I have - I need someone to scoop me up and tell me it's all okay, that I'm not a bumbling sack of sh*t. I can feel another stage of re-invention coming on - Hey, I got through phase one right?!

I'm sorry to be self-indulgent, but I know there are many of you here that will understand how I feel, I'm going back to read through some of the advice I so often dish out and take a slice of it for myself. Just a bit of a wobble I think.

Love Always

Vic and Pat

xxxx

20th February 2017

Monday... Oh Monday how I loath thee... Let's get one thing straight, Monday, You are NOT going to ruin my mood!

Let's talk about turning things around.

Dealing with different emotional challenges in life often leaves us feeling like we are wearing pants that are 3 sizes too small. They are uncomfortable, make us feel restricted and we know that shaking them off isn't going to be very pleasant. BUT... the feeling when you get them off is sheer delight, relief and you know never to try and get them on again.

Today I feel like those tiny bum pinchers are half way down my thighs, still uncomfy ... but nearly off!! I'm turning things around.

Now, if something in your life is affecting everything else you do for the worse, it's time to change that thing. Can you pin point one negative thing that is having an influence over you that you cannot control? I personally have a few but the main one is my total and utter lack of self-worth which leads to insecurity. Today marks the very day that I am TURNING THIS SH*T AROUND!!!!

I have been given a very clever tool by a very special person and that is to create a mentor of my mind - a facilitator to help me when I am filled with doubt. Each and every time a negative thought enters my head, there will be this constant uplifting voice telling me that I am brilliant, I am capable and I am going to succeed.

The main thing I am trying to establish, is what will be the end goal? My goals with Pat are not overly measurable but I would like to achieve greatness. I would like to do something this year that I look back on next year and feel proud of. Ideally, I would like to overcome all odds and complete a BE100 or even a NOVICE!! Remembering that this time last year, I couldn't even face getting on let alone doing a jump, I know I have already achieved so much - why stop there! I CAN DO THIS!!

Secondly, I would like to be a confident person, in control of my reactions and emotions. Just jotting these things down on here has made me feel positive, like I CAN do anything I set my mind to. We all can. WE CAN ALL ACHIEVE GREATNESS - one step at a time.

Let's go get it, start today - feel passionate and chase your dreams, we only have one chance to make our mark - take it - TAKE IT NOW!!

Love you all ... Get those knickers off!!!!!

Vic and Pat xxx

21st Feb 2017

I wrote this for anyone that feels like giving up on following their dreams;

When you feel like giving in,

You feel uneasy in your skin.

Just take a minute to unwind,

Count to ten and search your mind.

Find comfort and take confidence

And try to grasp some kind of sense.

Breathe in, breathe out and focus on

Success and just how far you've come.

Open up a brand new door,

Find one where no-one's keeping score.

There's only you, be proud, stand tall,

I'll catch you if you start to fall.

Dream big, take steps to tread your track

And remember – I've ALWAYS got your back.

xxx

24th February 2017

Boom boom boom... let me hear you say WAAAY-O....
(Tumbleweed for those born beyond the 80's!!)

It's only BLOODY FRIDAY!!! Pub night, no work for 2 days night... I am happy happy happy!! Channelling my inner positive person this week has made me feel blindingly fab. Here's something to work on this afternoon;

Stand up, get up off the bloody sofa, out of your office chair, out of the car and just for a minute (depending on who's watching - go to the toilet if you need to) - Stand on one leg, raise your fists to your arm pits and move your elbows up and down, give out a loud clucking noise and then sit back down - if you can do that without laughing at yourself, I will personally wear my pants on my head to the pub tonight!

One of the most beneficial things in life is being able to laugh at yourself. If you fall off (and you're not on the way to hospital), laugh about how your pants haven't been cut from your bare bum in public. Laugh when you forget your dressage test, only *you* will be able to remember the next move and stressing out isn't going to help your brain to find it! Laugh at your wrinkles, that spot on your chin, laugh at the grey hairs you keep finding and pulling out... Alright... Those are all mine, but you get my drift.

If you can master the art of laughing at yourself it will act as a shield to nasty chip p*ssers that ruin your day. Enjoy being alive, only *you* can control your mood - people can effect it momentarily, but *YOU* are in control - bloody well grab it by the horns <3

Weekend plans... Go on, get me the Imodium... That's right - I have a SHOW tomorrow. The leavings are loose, the palms are moist and I'm already wondering what is going in the flask! I have Combined Training at 9.36am, Dressage test and show jumping round and then home for lunch to do some writing! Nothingy day on Sunday, just chilling out.

What's on the cards for you this weekend? Hope you have a lovely one <3

Love Always

Vic & Pat

xxxx

February 25, 2017

Standard!! Leavings are Loose as a goose, sipping from the flask of courage ... here we go again xxxx

February 26, 2017

Hurrah!!!!! We survived another outing! So with the tail end of storm Doris licking out our heels yesterday, we trundled off to Coombelands Equestrian Centre for our first ever combined training♥ show. Up at the yard, having a mini meltdown about my missing hat silk and bridle number, trusty friends stepped in to assist! Plaited and ready to go, we hacked the 35 minutes to the scene of potential death.

Pat was unnervingly calm, warmed up without so much as a squeak- long may that reign!! Number 73 "you're in" oh Christ... I hate those two tiny words, she may as well have said "if you'd care to sign this 'consent to die' form". The bell sounded and four strides down the centre line and the horn sounds... what the cr*pper could I have possibly ballsed up this early on?! Oh that's right, I haven't taken the pony boots off!! Buggeration! It put me right off! Good ole' Daddy Carrot to the rescue, and we set off again.

He did a sweet test, nothing flashy, just correct.

On to the jumping, boots back on, we jumped the practice cross pole twice and the spread once and went in. It's enough, I know he can jump, whatever do I need to check again and again for?! So off we go in a nice rhythm, missed the stride to the first but he jumped so well 💜💜 he bashed number 10 which had a lot of people caught out but what a dear darling boy. He makes me feel like we can do anything.

So just one down, I waited for the results and I'm so glad we did. We came SECOND!!!! If I hadn't lost 2 points for those bloody boots being left on, we'd have sneaked in at number one!! We would have also done our first sub 30% test but alas a 30.2% for us today. I'm delighted with my best boy, he was perfect today. It was great to get that run out before our first 2017 BE next week too. YEP YOU HEARD RIGHT!!

Thank you everyone for your endless support, to Gaye and the team at Coombelands and to dearest Daddy Carrot for videoing our bobblings 😊😊 we got a lovely rosette and a bag of KM Elite goodies!!!!

March 2017

1st March 2017

TODAY, WE ARE CELEBRATING!!!!!!!

Thanks so, so much to all of you beautiful, wonderfully supportive and fabulous people that following my mumblings. I am so desperately proud to have attracted such a kind and helpful support network of non-chip p*ssers. I love you all.

Today, my beloved Diary of a Wimpy Eventer has reached a massive milestone of over 8000 people in just 5 months. I am so grateful and so proud of how far I have come in confidence, not just with my riding but with my writing too. I have so many of you on here to thank for that. You have believed in me, supported me through some of my darkest, terrified times and held my virtual hand at every show. I genuinely cherish every single comment, private message and photo that gets sent. Proof that none of us are alone. I have your back, just as you have mine.

Lots of love today and always <3 xxxx

2nd March 2017

It's twitchy bum time...

First BE event of 2017 Aston Le Walls - times are out. Holy Guacamole!!

3rd March 2017

Today I would like to tell you all a little tale of courage...

Let's roll back to July 2016... Every day at 3.30pm I would begin the battle. My heart would race, my toilet visits would increase and by 4.30pm when I finished work I could barely grip the car steering wheel through sweating palms. On arrival at the yard I would pray for an excuse; a missing shoe, rain, the wrong colour pants on - any excuse to not have to ride - I'd take it.

I was consumed by guilt, consumed by fear unable to see light at the end of the darkest tunnel I had ever been in.

Bit by bit I began re-inventing myself.

Each day we did a little more, dropped the dope a little more and hacked a little more, after 2 weeks the day loomed of our 'hunt ride' and I was more scared than I have been of anything for a long, long time. 2 hours later I was hacking home, grinning like never before. I had done it, we were alive and I was full to the brim with pride. We were courageous for the first time in years and what a feeling!

Ever since this day, I have tried to emulate that feeling. Conquering fear is the best feeling in the world, grab it with both hands. Be brave, do something courageous, the repayments you get far outweigh the terror I promise you. After 8 months of being unable to get my saddle out of the tackroom I made the decision to change the world. Just our world, the small bit of it that we take up and look at us now.

We still battle, not hourly or daily anymore, but certainly weekly! Striving for that feeling has been the very best adventure I could have ever wished for and long may it continue.

Please, trust me and take that leap of courage - however small. If it doesn't repay you the first time, don't you dare give up - it WILL repay you in the end and if it doesn't - It is most certainly not the end.

Love as always, Vic and Pat xxxxx

Sobbing at my desk again!! Cheeses!!!

4th March 2017

It's RAINED off!!! No first event of the season for us tomorrow. Three weeks to wait until the next one at Munstead and I've missed my run at 80... it's straight in at 90 for us!!

For the first time ever, I wasn't scared either... I'm now lunging Pat and sulking instead!!!

5th March 2017

So after Aston BE got cancelled, I had already decided to do something to get my adrenalin up, to scare myself just as I would have been going cross country today. Jumping at home is my scariest nemesis so that was that... decision made!!

We trundled down with Daddy Carrot, a camera and my Bravery Vest♥ (Point Two Pro Air) firmly clipped in, for some serious jumping action... started off with some poles, a cross pole and then a small up right before building the oxer of doom!! Gappy and large, my pony soared through the air like a podgy heron! We ballsed it a few times but what a feeling!!!!

Was I scared? Absolutely.

Did I scream murderously, balling bad instructions at my poor husband who was out there building jumps in the pissing rain? Yes I did!

But, did we die? Nope!

And do I now feel like jumping 90 cms will be a doddle? Hurrah...yes we bloody do!!

We jumped 1m15 today, our biggest jump to date, with no pant stains or death.

My lovely little horse tried so hard despite the horrid weather, what a brilliant day after the screaming disappointment of no BE party to go to!

xxxx

8th March 2017

Apologies in advance to all of those on here that are smuggling a todger in their trunks, but as it is International Women's Day, I am remarkably proud to say that on this page I have never ever encountered such support, loyalty and kindness between equestrian loving women in my whole life.

Ladies... Let's celebrate the fact that we like a moan, whether it be the weather, the fluff and crumbs that appear from nowhere in our handbags, the remarkable difference of going into one shop and being a size ten and then a size twenty in the shop next door. We get wrinkles, eventually, we get saggy bosoms, eventually. It is inevitable that we will all at some stage, buy a coloured eyeliner or funky hair dye on impulse and change our minds about reinventing ourselves on a lonely Saturday evening (and just eat a bar of Galaxy instead).

We are a wonderful breed - Here is today's mission if you care to accept it.....

Take a look at one (or more) of the wonderful women in your life and tell them why they are so special to you. A text, a PM, a call, pop over and see them. Let them know why they are brilliantly wonderful. Do they give the best hugs when you feel rotten? Do they text to make sure you're doing ok? Or do they just always have a knack of looking like a supermodel even when they are covered in hay and mud? Tell them. Make someone you care about feel wonderful, they deserve it after all.

One day, when we have nagged all the men to death or killed them off by making them build a new cross country jump in the pouring rain - we will need each other for survival...!

And while you're at it... bloody well go and look in the mirror again, like we did before - find one thing you love about yourself and say it out loud... be proud of who you are, there is no shame in tooting on your own trumpet, toot away my wonderful friends, toot like you mean it. Don't you dare feel guilty for feeling bloody fabulous about yourself. You are all so special - enjoy that feeling.

Have a wonderful day.

Love as always xxxxx

11th March 2017

Pat and I are pulling out all the stops to make sure we are in fine fettle for our first event of the season!!

We trundled off for a jumping lesson at Coombelands Equestrian Centre this morning with Russell Cooper.

I was, as usual, nervous as ever! I had a poorly tummy in the night and spent a good couple of hours with my head over the toilet which made me feel so bloody wobbly when mounting my spooky beast. Lucky for me, Pat jogged and spooked nearly all the way there which helped no end (NOT), but once we had warmed up and knuckled down to popping a little warm up jump, I had forgotten about my belly bugs.

Now, I have been riding 25 years, I have ridden around 300 different horses (give or take) and I have never really been able to see a stride to a fence or ride a decent canter at one!! And today I learnt why!!

Within 10 minutes, clever Russell asked me when I began looking at the fence? Gave an amazing example of peripheral vision and basically spanked my ass for losing focus... I do!!! That is exactly what I do, I lose focus. Constantly! Pat spooks, focus on the fence is lost! So with this in mind I began thinking about his feet and where they fell, miles away from the jump.

We put together a course of fences at 85/90ish and worked on the canter, I have learnt so much today. Lifting my belly button, riding with my contact on a level 2 - this is a BIG deal for me, I am usually gripping on like a monkey so if he does get strong, I have nowhere to go from already holding his mouth. The more nervous I am, the more I cling on and shut down the canter. Focus, forward, light hands, and it all just came together.

I felt capable and confident and totally loving being a brain sponge to the teachings of someone very good at their profession.

I was even brave enough to jump a few of the bigger ones at the end! Sadly there was no Daddy Carrot with his camera today, but fear not... this is the first of many I think. 🖤🖤🖤

15th March 2017

Good Morning All,

Firstly, I would like to make my apologies for being a little quiet of late. I have had a bout of heart palpitations that have made me pretty lethargic.

I wanted to touch on this and why I think I have them.

Stress, panic, worry, low confidence and fear. Something I have in equal measures at different times, add all of those together and they culminate in affecting your health and general living of life.

Now, on the surface of things, I appear (and feel, most of the time) happy, at ease and full of the joys of spring but occasionally, something darker creeps in. It consumes you. It takes over your focus and makes you feel as though you can't do anything worthwhile.

I am learning ways to keep this creepy darkness from sneaking its pork-pie head into my business. Day to day, if something makes you feel less than happy or makes you feel unfulfilled - work out a way to remove it. It will eat you up inside, not immediately but eventually.

As long as you have a plan to get away from the cause, this will be enough to maintain focus. I will admit, although I have a plan - this theory is failing me! I have a plan to write a book, to sell enough of them to be able to leave my full time marketing job. Maintaining focus is pivotal.

If there is something in your life that you have always wanted to do, don't leave life without doing it. You must grab inspiration where you can and if that's from me - well grab all you like. I am bloody well going to finish this book, I am going to make it a success and I am going to feel damn well proud of myself for taking that inspiration.

Take it, today. Make the plans, even loose Post-it note ones, and seriously - grab whatever you can and run like the wind. Worry not what people think about you or your plans - they are yours, not theirs. Be proud of yourself, do something to make yourself proud...

I'm back in the game today and I'm not going to lose focus <3

Love, as always - Vic & Pat xxxxx

17th March 2017

4.30pm on a FRIDAY.... My absolute FAVOURITE time of the week!!

WWWWWWAAAAAAAAAHHHHHHOOOOOOOOO!!!!!!!

Weekend plans are to prepare for Munstead BE90 next weekend (Literally soiling my skimpies over this one), learn the dressage test and jump something bigger than a twig. Going to see Beauty and the Beast tomorrow night which I need to practice the songs for (sorry fellow cinema goers)!!

I am also going to start getting our stuff sorted for our 2017 eventing debut, as there won't be much time what with my frequent underpant changes in the run up to D-Day BE DAY!!!

Some Daddy Carrot time is long overdue on Sunday too.

Oh and I got some beautiful things in the post today from my dearest sponsors Foxy Equestrian, I still pinch myself that I actually have SPONSORS at all!!!!!

20th March 2017

So all in all, we had a lovely weekend. I am totally terrified by the prospect of our first BE of 2017 THIS SATURDAY!!!!!

After the cancellation of my nice safe start in the BE80 at Aston Le Walls, I am now lumped with starting at Munstead and entered into the 90. I could literally cry at how bloody nervous I am again. My palpitations are terrible and my palms sweat whenever I think about walking the course or learning the test. I need a poo just writing this.

So, I thought I would try and outline my concerns in a hope that writing them down makes light of the situation!!

What is the main thing that I am scared of....?

EASY - The show jumping. It stands out as my most terrifying bit.

And why? Because it will be big (90 -95 is big for us) and on grass and I might lose my way or let my horse down or not kick in the right place or he might slip over or I might die. I JUST HATE IT. I hate it, hate it hate it. I feel all over the place, I feel like I'm inexperienced and all flopity poppity all over his back! I feel like he jumps really big and I get left behind, then get the next one wrong.

Resolution -

Jump more often, put them up to 95-1m and see that it is ok and that as long as I know we can do it, it'll be what it will be on the day.

The only way for me to stop worrying about something that may or may not happen, is to not think about it until absolutely necessary. I'm going to learn the dressage test tonight and practice that today. Then at least it takes my mind away from dying in a field.

I am secretly excited, I look forward to getting my boxes of kit ready, I love plaiting, doing my stud holes and making him look nice - years of being a groom I guess, but now I'm the jockey - it's VERY different!

So let's see how the week progresses, how many impromptu toilet visits I make and how many times I cry!!

Love as always my darling treasures,

Vic & Pat xxx

22nd March 2017

WEDNESDAY - Oh bloody rainy horrible hungover Wednesday!!

Impromptu pub visit last night! I started to get VERY excited about the next few weeks and fancied a cheeky Tuesday Tipple that turned into 3!! I have a thick head, my diet has truly lost its way and I have snapped at 3 idiots in the office already!

My nerves over Munstead on Saturday are lurking somewhere behind fluffy wine head and excited 'We're off Eventing!" head... For goodness sake - What will be will be!

I'd like to share a little story with you all today.

Now, almost 13 years ago, I was riding for a lovely family in Lincolnshire that despite not being massively well off, had a couple of horses in for me to compete and hunt. I was very lucky to have a very beautiful ex-racer with manners to die for, who I adored within an inch of his tiny hooves. He wasn't bold cross country or careful show jumping, he was wooden as a board in the dressage but we were flying in open classes at about a 1m, I think it's where I learnt to smile on a horse.

My dear boy was getting on and a second horse was bought to run alongside. Heading off to a local dealer, the owners came home with a 'throwaway' - you know those ones that no one wants, that they can't even dishonestly sell to an unsuspecting idiot. That is what arrived. He was poor, covered in scars and looked truly fed up.

6 weeks in, after a good feed and some love, I climbed aboard. Holy Moly, he was bloody awesome. He felt strong, and powerful and gave me goose bumps as soon as we skipped into trot. I gave him another couple of months of easy work and we went to enter

our first show. I looked high and low for the passport, and when I found it I almost fell over.

The thick passport had EVERY single international stamp box filled with countries you could only dream of visiting, he had travelled the world... I sat trawling the internet for the history of this beautiful animal that had been so carelessly thrown away.

His appearances included;

Sydney Olympics (2000)

Athens Olympics (2004)

BADMINTON 4*!!!! (2002) Shocker dressage and 2 poles down show jumping but fast clear XC!

24 Advanced level outings

8 x 3* runs all over Europe

And here I was show jumping 3ft at a local show!!!

He owed the world nothing, I did bits and bobs and pootled gaining SO much experience from the wisdom imparted by this brave and wonderful horse. He retired happy and grazing with mates in the field at home, not stood ragged in a dealer's throwaway bin.

Oh bloody hell, I'm crying again.

The moral of this heart wrenching story is to NEVER EVER, and I mean EVER, judge anything or anyone on face value. Give them time, take a step back and look for something beyond the exterior. Try to see the good in everything and everyone and you will live a much happier life, I promise. People (and horses) can give you the most wonderful of surprises, even when you least expect it.

Love as always xxx

23rd March 2017

Holy Smokes!!!!

Leavings are loose guys... leavings. are. loose. I have my times for MUNSTEAD!!! Time of expected death - 8.12 am

26th March 2017

So here it is..... Number 1. The first one of 2017 and the last one of this book.

Back to Friday, I was nervous as hell. Having to sit in a quiet office all day, not overly busy, made my nerves worse. I had so much to do post 4.30pm and I was getting increasingly tittery about wanting to run out the door and to the cross country course. On arrival at Munstead, I was pleasantly greeted by beautiful going, evening sun and one of my best mates to hold my hand around the course.

Now, I'm not a fan of course walking, it gives me plenty to worry about, I hated number 6 - a trappy yellow jump of mortality, number 10 - the owl hole of uncertainty and number 13 – big log with a bloody great ditch under it!! There was however, not enough time to worry too much as it was then 6pm and I had to pick up my hire lorry at 7!!! By 9.30pm Pat was plaited, the lorry was packed and we were in the pub for my last glass of wine before almost certain death!

4am... bloody 4am... the alarm was set for 5.30, why oh why are you awake this early!? Daddy Carrot was awake too!! Bugger it, we got up, made a cuppa, piled make up on (so no one can see how bloody green I am under it!!) and sat on the toilet until we needed to leave!!

Everything loaded up, at 6.15am we set off on our 45 minute trip to Munstead. We were the 5th lorry there!! I was 3rd to go in my section at 8.12am so relieved to see I wasn't too early or too late. - I am still very new to this whole process, unsure how much time to leave and not really clued up on etiquette yet!! Lit another ciggie, had a coffee and got him ready.

Ah cr*p, I was doing his studs, literally TREMBLING!! I was terrified at this stage, the worst I've been for a long time but I got on, warmed up and headed off into the arena to meet my maker!! Now, I smile. You know I do. I smile like Miss UK on drugs, but it seems eventing judges haven't taken us too seriously in the past maybe for this reason. So my new tactic was to ride in a much more 'prelim' frame and not smile quite so much.... looking back at the photos, there are just somethings you can't change!!! I beamed like a retard the whole way through!! I felt it deserved a 31, I'd have been happy with that.

Next up - the 'sh*t yourself phase'. I really do dislike show jumping. It's too easy to mess up, I'm very inexperienced at it, I get tense and scared and I just want to get off now please!!! But, he warmed up so bloody well. I remembered everything from my lesson two weeks ago, didn't shut the canter down, BRILLIANT!!! In the ring however, apparently someone ever so discreetly, gave me an epidural because by all accounts I was paralysed from the waist down!!!! And clinging on like a monkey on his last banana, I rode appalling around what was actually a VERY nice course! I really did look like a total bloody limpet. I deserved the two poles we demolished, well and truly. But I came out smiling, mostly because it was over, but also because I got a 26 dressage, kindly announced as I sailed over fence one!!!!!!!

Phew.... that's the worst bit done!! Not likely.... all of a sudden, I'm cr*pping it again!! No time, no time... get changed, get on and wander down to the death zone waving my husband goodbye. I jumped a couple of practice fences that he backed off like a b*stard at. He is not a confident cross country horse yet, so I have to pretend to be a confident cross country rider that shows him the way …like hell!!

Start box, oh how I loath thee. "You've got 10 seconds" has to be the single most terrifying four words I face in life. Holy Moses, off we go. Sailed the first, sticky wicket at the second. Nearly had a stop but that dear horse does go if I tell him enough and go he did!! 3, 4, 5 went by with nothing to report - 6 I barely kicked I was so bloody scared of it... he jumped it for me. He took over for that split second, if I wasn't about to remove a lung from my mouth at this stage, I'd have sobbed with pride. 7, 8, 9, nothing to report apart from my lack of fitness. 10, I needed a rest at but Holy McOwlhole was coming to get us, he backed off a touch but went sailing through no problems. 11, 12, all flying, 13 that bloody great ditch.... forget it, I lifted his head, kicked like stink and we soared it, so big I almost left out of the rear exit!!! The rest of the course jumped beautifully, over the last and galloping through those final sets of red and white flags, I burst with love, pride and sheer elation. We've done it boy, we've done it!! (I can barely see to type, crikey it's emotional).

I seriously cannot put into words what this means for me to be able to be doing this. I've come from the darkest place of fear to get here; here finishing this 1st event of the season, safe, alive and happier than ever.

I have to say, there are so so many people involved that make it so truly special. Yesterday my husband made the world's best groom, best friend and best Daddy Carrot I could have ever wished for. My darling friends that surprised me with how wonderfully supportive people can be. My sponsors, I mean, I feel odd even writing that but boy did we look and feel the bloody big balls yesterday!! My yard chums, the preparation that goes in for weeks leading up to eventing season, they really have been so helpful. I can't tell you how amazing I feel right now.

Today we are giving back to the sport that I have fallen so madly in love with, Daddy Carrot and I are fence judging! But not before I go and give my horse the biggest squeeze of his life. Thank you all for everything, you too, are the reason we came 7th yesterday.... oh wait... yep you heard it right... a 26 dressage and 8 show jumping with a clear inside the time cross country, meant that we attended prize giving, got a big fat rosette and a cheque for £30!!! Bloody elated doesn't even come close!!!!

Love as always

Vic and Pat xxxxxxx

So that's that, the first step in my year long journey to find the biggest pair of balls I can. I LOVED every second of that feeling after the event, this is what keeps me motivated to enter the next one. It doesn't mean I am any less scared or any less nervous, it just means that like all of us, I am in search of the holy grail of 'post cross country exhilaration' (the non-death kind). Please follow your dreams, please be proud of everything you do. Remember only 10 months ago, I couldn't even get on my horse. ANYTHING is possible if you focus, stay positive and keep a handle on the fear and you CAN do this, I promise.

Turn the page - there is a list of things for you to remember, things to remind yourself of. Tear it out, fold it up and put it in your purse, on your fridge, somewhere you can see it daily. These things will keep you going when you have a moment of wobbly weakness, when you need it most. Read them – out loud if you can - keep in mind those things and I promise you will get there. If I can, then you can too.

Important things to remember

Those that mind don't matter and those that matter don't mind. Please keep that in mind when people p*ss on your chips!

Surround yourself with people that either couldn't give a sh*t, ones that would give their last sh*t to see you succeed, or the ones that don't know what sh*t you're doing.

Be brave, enjoy it and love the life you have - don't wish you were someone else, one day you might be and you might not be happier at all.

Be proud of where you are right now at this time of life, look to the future with hope, not dread. Be bold in your decisions to better that hopeful life.

The moral of the story is - if things don't go your way, it wasn't your way to go.

You will NEVER stop rivalry, jealousy or bitterness that is caused by the resentment of other people's success. – bloody well rise above it.

Work hard for the things that matter, don't lose focus, and be the best that you can be at those things. Don't make excuses for not working as hard as you could, because only you will suffer in the end.

If you feel down, find out the cause and make a plan... baby steps remember, soon you will be wondering what the problem was!

Be proud of who you are, don't always try to be different, you are already brilliant enough.

Enjoy being alive, only *you* can control your mood - people can effect it momentarily, but *YOU* are in control - bloody well grab it by the horns.

Be brave, do something courageous, the repayments you get far outweigh the terror I promise you.

If there is something in your life that you have always wanted to do, don't leave life without doing it. You must grab inspiration where you can and if that's from me - well grab all you like.

Worry not what people think about you or your plans - they are yours, not theirs.

Love as always,

Vic and Pat xx